BACK HOME

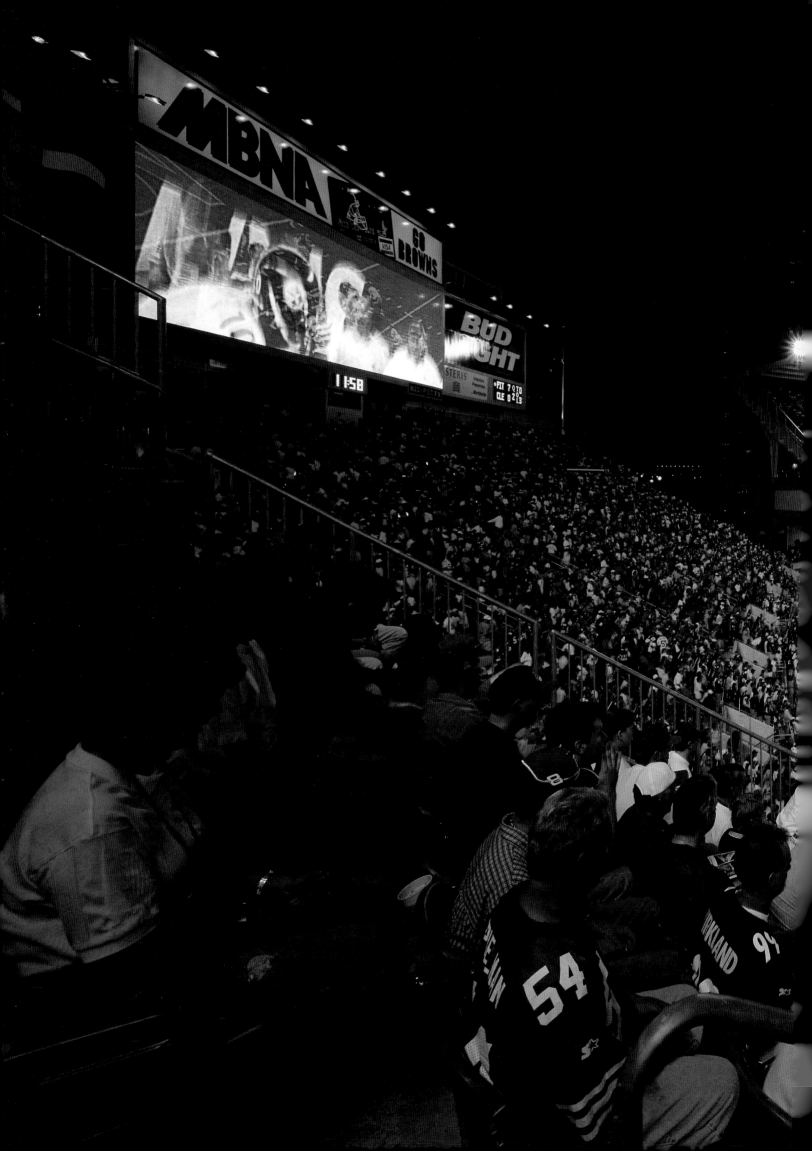

BACK HOME

VOLUME I
The Rebirth of the Cleveland Browns

Editor
Tim Graham

Design
Tom Morgan

Associate Editor
Rich Exner

Senior Writer
Dan Coughlin

Contributing Writers
Steve Herrick
Fred Greetham

Senior Photographer
Ron Kuntz

Contributing Photographers
Janine Exner
Roger Mastroianni
Stephen S. Counsel
Elizabeth Fulford Schiau
John H. Reid III

WOODFORD PRESS

Printed in Canada.

Book and cover design: Tom Morgan,
Blue Design, www.bluedes.com

Library of Congress Catalog Card Number
available upon request.
ISBN: 0-942627-69-5

Distributed by Andrews McMeel Publishing,
Kansas City, MO.

Woodford Press
5900 Hollis Street, Suite K
Emeryville, CA 94608

C. David Burgin, Editor and Publisher
Daniel C. Ross, CEO and Publisher
William F. Duane, Senior Vice President

Associate Publishers:
Franklin M. Dumm
William W. Scott, Esq.
William B. McGuire, Esq.

PAGES 2 AND 3: Opening Night against Pittsburgh,
September 12, 1999.

PAGE 4: Exterior of Cleveland Browns Stadium.

RIGHT: Fans pass through turnstiles to enter
Stadium.

PAGES 8 AND 9: Players race off the field through
a crowd of photographers and reporters after
the first home preseason game against
Minnesota on August 21, 1999.

PAGE 10: Tim Couch in action against New England
on October 3, 1999.

PAGES 12 AND 13: View from the press box.

Contents

Introduction
Family, Religion and the Browns

My romance with the Cleveland Browns began during the 1960s, growing up in small-town Ohio where football ruled. Friday nights belonged to the high schools, and Saturday to the Ohio State Buckeyes. In those days the Bucks were rarely on live television. As I went from home to home making collections on my paper route, families raked the leaves and listened to the games on transistor radios. Rarely did I escape the voice of Marv Homan, speaking live from high above Ohio Stadium. The best part of the weekend, however, was saved for last. Sundays belonged to the Cleveland Browns. ➤

My father was a United Methodist minister, and the Browns caused him to learn the importance of using the clock. In fact, it was partly because of the Browns and television that many churches moved the starting time of their main worship services from 11 to 10:45 a.m. The extra 15 minutes made it easier for the congregation to get home and finish Sunday dinner before the kickoff. My earliest memory of ever missing church dates to November 7, 1965, when I was 11 and attended my first Browns game. We were living in Bucyrus, and I sold enough newspaper subscriptions to win a bus trip to Cleveland to see the

The great Jim Brown, who played from 1957 through 1965, set the standard by which all NFL running backs are measured.

Browns. It was a typically gray November morning when my mother, who was eight months pregnant, drove me over to the Route 30 exit off I-71 near Mansfield, where I met a chartered bus full of newspaper carriers bound for Municipal Stadium.

The Browns defeated the Philadelphia Eagles, 38-34, and Jim Brown rushed for 131 yards. Years later, in Houston, I had the opportunity to meet Frank Ryan and he recalled that game. He remembered not feeling his best. It seems the studious Dr. Ryan had had a few too many the night before with one of his friends on the visiting team.

I share these recollections not because they're unique but because they're typical of ones I've shared with Browns fans from coast to coast. When I sat down with Carmen Policy before the 1999 season, he told me how his wife, Gail, helped him come to understand the intensity of devotion that so many millions of people feel for the Browns. She explained how her family would attend Mass, stop at the bakery for a couple of fresh loaves of bread afterward, share Sunday dinner and clean the dishes before sit-

Frank Ryan, who wore number 13, threw three touchdown passes to Gary Collins in a 27–0 upset of the heavily favored Baltimore Colts to win the NFL championship on December 27, 1964. It was the Browns' fourth NFL title and the last time Cleveland fans would celebrate a league championship during the 20th century.

ABOVE: Christopher Zawadzki of Parma was 4 when he got his first look at the Browns during their 1999 training camp in Berea.

LEFT: Perhaps the rabbit's foot made the difference as the Browns won their 1999 debut performance in the Hall of Fame Game in Canton on August 9, 1999.

ting down as a family to watch the Browns. "Family. Church. Browns," Policy said. "And it all came together for me."

Of course, some might question the order of priorities. I remember one cold Sunday morning when the heat wasn't working right at the church. Several parishioners asked my dad if it might be a good idea to cancel services. "It wouldn't stop anyone from going out to watch the Browns," he snapped. "But Dad," I explained, "people come to church to pray to God. They go to the Stadium to worship the Browns."

So when David Burgin and Dan Ross, co-owners of Woodford Publishing, asked me to help them produce these books, I couldn't say no. They too have roots in Ohio and grew up cheering for the Browns. For all of us, this has been a labor of love.

Back Home is a tribute to the return of the Browns to Cleveland, and the construction of a $283 million house of worship for the team and its fans. It's a story born of heartbreak but sustained by an enduring legacy of pride ingrained in a great city and its people. It's a story of boundless hope and promise for the new millennium. "We're not an expansion team," Policy said in Canton on the night the Browns were reborn. "We're the Cleveland Browns." Every fan knows what he meant. The Browns are indeed back home.

— Tim Graham

"I want to send a message, a message to everyone who ever made fun of Cleveland. A message to anyone who ever told a Cleveland joke or laughed at a Cleveland joke. You can now officially shut up!"

— DREW CAREY

1. THE KICKOFF

Cleveland rocks, Cleveland rocks!

BY TIM GRAHAM

The scoreboard at the end of the game said 43-0 in favor of Pittsburgh, but this one belonged to Cleveland. It was much more than a football game, and the real winners were the city of Cleveland and legions of devoted Browns fans who refused to quit. The real story wasn't the game, but the fact that there was a game.

Long after the details — the score and the grim reality that the first touchdown in the beautiful new Cleveland Browns Stadium was scored by Kordell Stewart of the rival Steelers — become fodder for trivia buffs, the evening of September 12, 1999, will be remembered as one of Cleveland's proudest moments. ➤

For a city that endured years as the butt of jokes on national television, a city that became known as the one place in America where water burned, the evening represented the culmination of a most remarkable chapter in a renaissance that returned Cleveland to glory.

No one summed up the essence of the occasion better than Drew Carey, the comedian and television star and native Clevelander who addressed the crowd before the teams took the field. "I want to send a message, a message to everyone who ever made fun of Cleveland. A message to anyone who ever told a Cleveland joke or laughed at a Cleveland joke. You can now officially shut up, because Cleveland rocks!" Carey said. "Cleveland rocks! Cleveland rocks!"

Indeed, Cleveland stood at the edge of the new millennium as the envy of chambers of commerce everywhere, the home of one of the world's greatest urban success stories. It is a story that transcends sports and goes to the heart the community's soul.

Back in 1982, when northeastern Ohio's unemployment rate was mired in double digits and many were giving up hope, a displaced steelworker encapsulated the region's despair by saying, "If the Communist Russians marched into town today, I'd sit on the curbstone and laugh like hell."

Even then, though, the seeds of Cleveland's revival were being planted. Dick Celeste, who was elected governor of Ohio that year, not only owed his victory to the city's Democratic base, he truly loved the place. He loved the Indians and Browns and appreciated the charm

of Municipal Stadium. But he knew it wouldn't last forever.

It's impossible to say exactly when Cleveland's renaissance began. There were encouraging signs downtown and in the adjoining Flats by the mid-1980s. But if you

PAGE 21: Ronnie Powell secured his place in history by grabbing the opening kickoff in the first game at Cleveland Browns Stadium, a preseason contest against Minnesota on August 21, 1999.

PAGE 22: Comedian Drew Carey, a Cleveland native, drew a thunderous ovation when he addressed the crowd before the first regular-season game, on September 12, 1999.

LEFT: Defensive back Tim McTyer was among the many Browns players who acknowledged the fans in the Dawg Pound on August 21, 1999.

RIGHT: The Browns race onto their new home field for the first time, August 21, 1999.

had to point to one thing, it might be the fact that Celeste and George Voinovich, the city's Republican mayor at the time, were able to put aside partisan differences and work to make Cleveland better.

So by the time the old Browns played their last game in Municipal Stadium, on December 17, 1995, Cleveland was a vastly different city from what it was a decade earlier. Some of the most visible new landmarks included Jacobs Field, Gund Arena, the Great Lakes Science Museum and the Rock and Roll Hall of Fame. And the river that caught fire? Pleasure boats crowd the Cuyahoga on summer weekends, and thousands of people are drawn to restaurants and bars along the water's edge.

Such a record of success made the loss of the Browns even more impossible to accept. And the reality is that no one, from Mayor Michael White to the fans in the Dawg Pound, ever did accept it. Thanks to their persistence, Cleveland has a new monument on the lakefront and a new football team that is in a position to build on the rich tradition of its predecessor.

The old Browns had Lou Groza, a rookie in the team's first year back in 1946, whose field goal in the final seconds gave the Browns the 1950 NFL championship in their first season as a member of the league. The new Browns still have Lou Groza, standing watch with former teammate Gene Hickerson during the stadium groundbreaking ceremonies on a blustery spring day in 1997, and participating in the ceremonial coin toss before the 1999 opening game.

Like just about everything connected to the opening game itself, the Browns lost the toss. This wouldn't be like the Browns' debut in 1946, when they blew away the visiting Miami Seahawks 44-0 and cruised to the first of four consecutive titles in the old All-America Football Conference. Nor would it be like the Browns' first game in the NFL, when they went into Philadelphia on September 16, 1950, and decimated the defending-champion Eagles, 35-10.

Pittsburgh's dominance brought the 73,138 fans down to earth. Cleveland gained just 40 yards offensively during the game, picking up just two first downs. The Steelers gained 460 yards and earned 32 first downs. Afterward there wasn't much Cleveland Coach Chris Palmer could say except, "We have no place to go but up."

The new Browns, who entered the league on a firm footing financially under the ownership of Al Lerner and structurally under the direction of President and CEO Carmen Policy, are expected to rise quickly. "We are here with a very, very simple mandate," Policy said. "Build the best sports organization in America, make sure it lives here in Cleveland and make sure it does very well."

The defensive unit stopped the Steelers early but got little chance to rest as the Browns offense picked up just two first downs, both in the first quarter.

Chris Gardocki's Opening Night kickoff sailed into the end zone for a touchback, one of the few bright spots for the Browns in a game that went downhill from there.

What it means to be a Browns fan

BY DAN COUGHLIN

You come in every imaginable size, shape, pigmentation, ethnic origin, social strata and educational background.

You are a 6-year-old boy clinging to your father's hand and you are an 86-year-old man clutching your grandson's arm.

You are a 350-pound man wearing a dog mask and a number 98 jersey. You are a 98-pound woman who has attended every Browns home game since 1946.

You are Hank Aaron sitting unnoticed in the Dawg Pound between an electrician from the city and a plumber from the country.

You scored 1,400 on your SAT but you reverse the evolutionary current every other Sunday in the fall when you sit in the rain and bark like a dog.

You can still hear the voices of Bob Neal, Bill McColgan, Gib Shanley and Nev Chandler calling out the names of Otto Graham, Jim Brown, Leroy Kelly and Ozzie Newsome. No one thinks you are crazy.

You are a Browns fan. You predate dog faces, dog bones and dog biscuits. Carbon dating establishes your birth in 1946, before television, before *Sports Illustrated*, before the AFL, WFL, USFL, Pete Rozelle and Howard Cosell.

You are tough and you cherish that image. Your team plays on real grass, not a plastic carpet, although sometimes it turns to mud and then

You remember Phipps to Pitts, the Kardiac Kids and Bernie Kosar drawing a play in the dirt in his final game as a Brown against the Denver Broncos.

to ice. An ideal football afternoon includes 50-mile-an-hour winds, driving sleet and mud deep enough to bury a panel truck. You always knew that when the airport was shut down and the interstates closed, Leroy Kelly would rush for 150 yards.

You were there in January 1981, when the windchill factor plunged to 8,000 degrees below zero, slightly colder than the temperature on Uranus, and you came down with frostbite, hypothermia, pneumonia, and The Plague. You passed a kidney stone at halftime. And you were at work the next day.

Supposedly a psychological defense mechanism dulls the most painful experiences from the memory, but every Browns fan knows this is nonsense. Brown-and-orange hair shirts should be officially licensed

Jeff Baranuk of Middleburg Heights on the first day of training camp in Berea.

NFL merchandise because you remember Pat Summerall's 49-yard field goal through the snow in the last game of the 1958 season in Yankee Stadium. You remember "Red Right 88." You remember "The Drive" and "The Fumble" and "I had no choice."

Your heart has been in the shop more times than a '46 Chevy.

But you also remember the euphoria of Lou Groza's field goal to win the 1950 NFL championship game and Frank Ryan's three touchdown passes to Gary Collins to win the 1964 championship game. You remember Phipps to Pitts, the Kardiac Kids and Bernie Kosar drawing a play in the dirt in his final game as a Brown against the Denver Broncos.

You also remember some of the damnedest things. Such as Cliff Lewis — who grew up on Belle Avenue in Lakewood, exactly seven miles from Cleveland Stadium — starting the Browns' first official league game at quarterback and combining with Mac Speedie on the

first official touchdown pass.

You remember meeting Groza at a church function and staring at his right foot as you shook his hand.

If you are Mike Holland, you remember writing a letter to Otto Graham inviting him to visit your St. Luke's grade school team practice and your astonishment when he did— on his way home from his own practice.

You are not perfect. You are slow to forgive and quick to avenge. Your enemies list is longer than Nixon's. Sam Huff, Bobby Layne, Terry Bradshaw and John Elway are merely the most notorious. You even hated the Chicago Rockets and the Los Angeles Dons, for Pete's sake!

You are slightly paranoid because you believe there is a conspiracy to exclude Gene Hickerson, Jim Ray Smith, Bob Gain and Gary Collins from the Hall of Fame.

Like Dick Ziska and Leonard Gibel, you have a penchant for symmetry. In 1946, Ziska and Gibel, both 9 years old, rode the No. 25 Madison streetcar downtown from Lakewood to attend the Browns' first game in the All-America Football Conference. In 1995, Ziska and Gibel, both age 58, rode the No. 25 Madison bus downtown to see the Browns' final game before the continuum was interrupted.

You also are an idealist. You expect each new coach to be as innovative as Paul Brown, as kindly as Blanton Collier and as quotable as Sam Rutligiano. Otto Graham led the Browns to 10 straight championship games and won seven of them. If you do not think it can be done again, you are not a Browns fan.

"Imagine you were a Frenchman, and they came along and uprooted the Eiffel Tower from its moorings and dropped it down in Germany. Well, it's not much of an exaggeration to say that's exactly what a Cleveland Browns fan felt like following the 1995 season when Art Modell took his team and moved to Baltimore."

—AL MICHAELS OF ABC, AUGUST 9, 1999

Cleveland Browns
starting lineup

SEASON OPENER
AGAINST PITTSBURGH,
SEPTEMBER 12, 1999

Defense

94—Derrick Alexander, Left End
67—John Jurkovic, Left Tackle
93—Jerry Ball, Right Tackle
99—Hurvin McCormack, Right End
53—John Thierry, Linebacker
58—Wali Rainer, Linebacker
95—Jamir Miller, Linebacker
24—Corey Fuller, Left Cornerback
38—Antonio Langham, Right Cornerback
23—Marquez Pope, Strong Safety
22—Tim McTyer, Free Safety

Offense

85—Kevin Johnson, Wide Receiver
75—Lomas Brown, Left Tackle
71—Jim Pyne, Left Guard
64—Dave Wohlabaugh, Center
79—Scott Rehberg, Right Guard
77—Orlando Brown, Right Tackle
82—Irv Smith, Tight End
86—Leslie Shepherd, Wide Receiver
11—Ty Detmer, Quarterback
42—Terry Kirby, Running Back
44—Marc Edwards, Fullback

The importance of the Browns to Cleveland

BY DAN COUGHLIN

Years ago somebody with a string of uppercase initials after his name introduced the theory of internal clocks, and we readily bought into it. The internal clock tells us when to get up, when to get hungry, when to get tired and when to go to bed. There are morning people and there are night people. It seemed logical, and personal experience suggested it was true.

In Cleveland, people are born with internal compasses. The compass tells you who you are and what you are. You are either an East Sider or a West Sider. People take great pride in their compass points, especially the West Siders, who are perceived as ignorant, downtrodden oafs.

All the great museums, most of the universities and the most exclusive country clubs are on the East Side. The fabulous mansions and estates are in the eastern suburbs. Within Greater Cleveland's predominant Irish community, East Side Irish are "lace curtain" and the West Side Irish are "shanty."

The two sides are clearly divided by the Cuyahoga River, which generally meanders south from Lake Erie. More accurately, the river flows north into Lake Erie, but the point is that the river is a psychological divider.

LEFT: Otto Graham, one of the greatest students the game has known, led the Browns to championship game appearances during each of his 10 seasons, 1946-1955. This photo was taken in August 1955, as he reconsidered his decision to retire after the 1954 season. He returned for one final championship encore.

For half a century, the Browns were the only psychological bridge that unified the largest metropolitan area between New York City and Detroit.

The Stadium itself, located on the lakefront between West Third Street and East Ninth Street, actually straddles the East Side and the West Side. One end zone is in the East Side; the other end zone is in the West Side. According to the post office map, the end zones are in different zip codes.

Only the Browns brought this divided city together. The Indians abdicated that responsibility when they allowed a maniacal carpetbagger general manager named Frank Lane to trade away Rocky Colavito on the eve of opening day in 1960. The Indians were not heard from again for 35 years.

Even during Cleveland's darkest days, the Browns were a sliver of light, a ray of hope.

The 1960s were Cleveland's banana-peel decade. The city fell on hard times. Imperceptibly at first, jobs started to evaporate. Downtown theaters closed. Nightlife went silent, except for the sounds of sirens and gunshots during the race riots.

The 1970s became a high-speed plunge into a civic abyss. A spark from a hotbox on a freight train ignited trash near a trestle that crossed the Cuyahoga River. The fire spread to the wooden timbers of the trestle, which touched off floating oil and chemicals that had collected under the trestle. It was not a major fire. As a matter of fact, it was a small fire. But pictures suggested that the river was on fire. The Cuyahoga became known and the river that burned, a once-in-a-millennium event. Cleveland's national image was scorched.

By the end of the decade Cleveland suffered the humiliation of default on its debts when conservative bankers, who lived in the fancy eastern suburbs, foreclosed in order to spank an aggressive, idealistic young mayor, who lived on Cleveland's humble near West Side.

Cleveland was an emotional wreck. But through all this torment,

Fans surround the Browns as they leave the field after winning their first championship, of the All-America Football Conference, in 1946. The Browns defeated the New York Yankees, 14–9. The Browns were the only champions the AAFC ever knew, and the league disbanded after the 1949 season.

LEFT: Jim Brown transcended race and replaced Rocky Colavito as Cleveland's hero, leading the Browns to their most recent of four NFL championships in 1964.

ABOVE: Leroy Kelly, who followed in Brown's footsteps, put up numbers that secured him a place in the Pro Football Hall of Fame.

the Browns held three-hour therapy sessions each Sunday afternoon in the fall.

Jim Brown transcended race when he replaced Rocky Colavito as the city's hero and the Browns returned to glory in 1964 when they won the NFL championship. The Browns played in the NFL championship game again the next year, but lost in Green Bay, a loss that was easy to rationalize. A blizzard struck Green Bay the night before the game and it took the Browns almost two hours to make the harrowing bus ride through the snow from their motel 30 miles outside Green Bay to Lambeau Field. Players believe they left their game on the bus.

The Browns made a run at the NFL championship again in 1968 and '69 when they rallied around Bill Nelsen, a garrulous, swashbuckling quarterback with gimpy knees. They fell short again, losing the 1968 NFL championship game to Baltimore and losing in 1969 to Minnesota. They were one victory shy of the Super Bowl. There was always the belief, however, that they would win it next year. For 14 straight home games from 1968 to the early part of 1970, the Browns attracted sellout crowds in excess of 80,000.

Bill
NELSEN
CLEVE. BROWNS ● QUARTERBACK

Beyond the emotional lift the Browns provided, there were measurable economic benefits.

On Monday mornings during the football season, newspaper circulation increased. Fans devoured every printed word. Under the leadership of innovative sports editor Hal Lebovitz, Cleveland's morning paper, *The Plain Dealer*, began trumpeting Browns' game stories with eight-column headlines on page one, which normally was allocated only for wars, politics and plane crashes.

Sometimes the Browns did crash and burn — they did frequently in the 1970s — but by the end of the decade a charismatic coach from Brooklyn and a Hollywood-handsome quarterback from southern California merged to create the Kardiac Kids.

Thus began the apparel craze. Sporting goods stores could not keep enough number 17 Brian Sipe jerseys in stock, or number 34 Greg Pruitts, number 43 Mike Pruitts, number 82 Ozzie Newsomes, number 85 Dave Logans, number 33 Reggie Ruckers, number 35 Calvin Hills or number 77 Lyle Alzados. Some people even wore number 73 Doug Diekens.

The Kardiac Kids had personality. They transfused a city that was starving economically and bleeding to death from the gaping wounds of political wars.

Players hosted Monday-night bar shows which played to packed houses in saloons, restaurants and motel lounges. Bartenders were able to send their children to private schools and waitresses moved up to midsize cars.

By the late 1980s a new cast of characters wore the Brown and Orange and the frenzy incredibly increased. Quarterback Bernie Kosar was barely old enough to vote and fanatics talked of running him for mayor. The Browns fell one game short of the Super Bowl three times in the late '80s, when people actually camped outside the Stadium in freezing weather to buy those precious playoff tickets.

As an emotional and economic catalyst, the Browns were the most significant force in Cleveland since Andrew Carnegie and John D. Rockefeller.

The ultimate unification of East and West was consummated with explosive force on November 6, 1995, when Art Modell stood on a makeshift dais in a Baltimore parking lot and uttered those infamous words, "I had no choice."

In Cleveland the emotional and economic fusion raised a mushroom cloud which eventually blanketed the entire National Football League.

From the ruins of catastrophe the new Browns emerged, in a glittering edifice that still straddles two zip codes, one end zone on the West Side, the other on the East Side.

Brian Sipe, who quarterbacked the Kardiac Kids, still holds most of the Browns' career passing records, including most pass attempts (3,439), most completions (1,944) and most touchdown passes (154).

Ozzie Newsome, the Wizard of Oz, caught 662 passes during his Hall of Fame career, more than anyone in Browns history and twice as many as the 331 caught by the runner-up, Gary Collins.

Otto who?

Here are 32 questions to test the knowledge of any Browns fan. If you do not know why there are 32, do not try to take the kickoff out of the end zone. Please find the answers under "Trivial pursuing," on page 185.

1. Who was the starting quarterback for the Cleveland Browns in their first regular-season game in 1946, their inaugural season in professional football?

2. Before Ozzie Newsome in 1999, who was the last Browns inductee in the Hall of Fame?

3. Before they began play as the Cleveland Browns in 1946, the team briefly had a different nickname. What was it?

4. When Chris Palmer was an offensive coordinator for the New Jersey Generals in the USFL, what onetime Browns quarterback did he coach?

Otto Graham runs for 12 yards during the 1950 NFL championship game, as Dante Lavelli gets in the face of Rams defender Bob Boyd. The Browns won 30-28 on a Lou Groza field goal with less than a minute to play to capture their first NFL title.

Leroy Kelly.

5. From 1952 through 1974 the Browns held their annual training camp at Hiram College. Where was the first training camp home of the Browns?

6. Lou Groza is best known for wearing No. 76. What other number did he wear?

7. With three enshrinees, Cleveland is the native home to more Hall of Famers than any Ohio city. Name the three.

8. Who is credited with inventing the face mask for football helmets?

9. The first Super Bowl was played after the 1966 season. Of the 15 teams in the NFL that year, which ones have never been to the big dance?

10. The Browns were the only champions the All-America Football Conference ever had, winning all four years of the league's existence. Whom did the Browns defeat in the championship games?

11. Twelve Browns in 1986 took their shot at acting, starring in "Masters of the Gridiron," a short feature about ancient warriors in a quest for a Super Bowl ring. Who was the guest (non-football) star?

12. Which Browns players in "Masters of the Gridiron" can you name based on these screen names? Hairstone, Dixonus, Golican, Clayrock, Mackmaulus, Bynthor, Baabarian, Pagelion, The Magical Wizard, Fike the Fierce, Nikoli and Puzzmong.

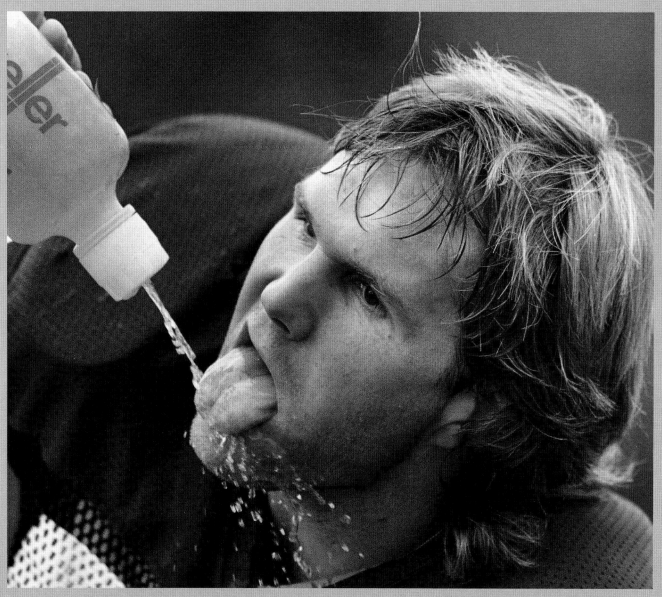

Clay Matthews.

Dub Jones, Ed Modzelewski, Otto Graham and Ray Renfro were even more awesome on dry land. The Browns practiced in the snow in late December 1955 before traveling to Los Angeles to defeat the Rams and win their second consecutive NFL title.

13. Thirty-five states, the District of Columbia, and Guatemala, Canada, Italy, Bavaria, Norway and Honduras have natives in the Pro Football Hall of Fame. Name the states that have the most in the Hall of Fame.

14. Which player from a Cleveland area high school scored a point for the Browns as a replacement player in 1987?

15. Which Browns defensive back, drafted in the first round in 1972, attended Sandusky High School?

16. Who started at quarterback in the first game after Bernie Kosar was cut?

17. Who replaced Don Cockroft as placekicker to begin the 1981 season?

18. What team did the Browns play in their annual Saturday night home game in the 1960s?

19. How many times have the Browns won the NFL championship?

20. The Browns finished the 1993 season with a 7-9 record. What was the Browns record after eight games when Bill Belichick released Bernie Kosar.

21. Lou Groza kicked the old-fashioned way, straight on. Who was the last straight-on (non-soccer-style) field-goal kicker for the Browns?

22. What national college running-back award is named after a player who was once the property of the Browns?

Lou Groza in 1964 with some of the many mementos from his Hall of Fame career. Three weeks after this photo was taken he would kick two field goals in the Browns' 27-0 upset of the Baltimore Colts for the NFL championship, the Browns' fourth and final one of the 20th century.

23. What future Browns starting quarterback was the second pick, behind Jim Brown, for the team in the 1957 draft?

24. What future Browns head coach was the team's No. 1 selection in the 1958 draft?

25. What future Hall of Famer was a seventh-round draft pick by the Browns in 1962?

26. Who was picked by the Browns ahead of Ozzie Newsome in the first round of the 1978 draft?

27. Which college leads the Browns in draft picks all-time?

28. What barrier did Marion Motley and Bill Willis break when they played for the Browns in 1946?

29. Lou Groza led the All-America Football Conference in scoring his first year with the Browns, and college football's annual award for the best kicker in the nation is named after Groza. How many times did he lead Ohio State in scoring?

30. Cuyahoga County voters in 1995 approved an extension of a special tax on cigarettes and alcohol to pay for the new Cleveland Browns Stadium. Did voters have a say in the construction of Municipal Stadium, completed in 1931?

31. The Browns had 10 head coaches before their return to the field in 1999. How many had career winning records?

Bill Willis

32. Who was the first player signed to play for the Cleveland Browns team that began play in 1946?

"We will go out there on Sunday to win,
not just to play."

—AL LERNER

Welcome
Cleveland
BROWNS FANS
RAMPS to NORTH COAST HARBOR

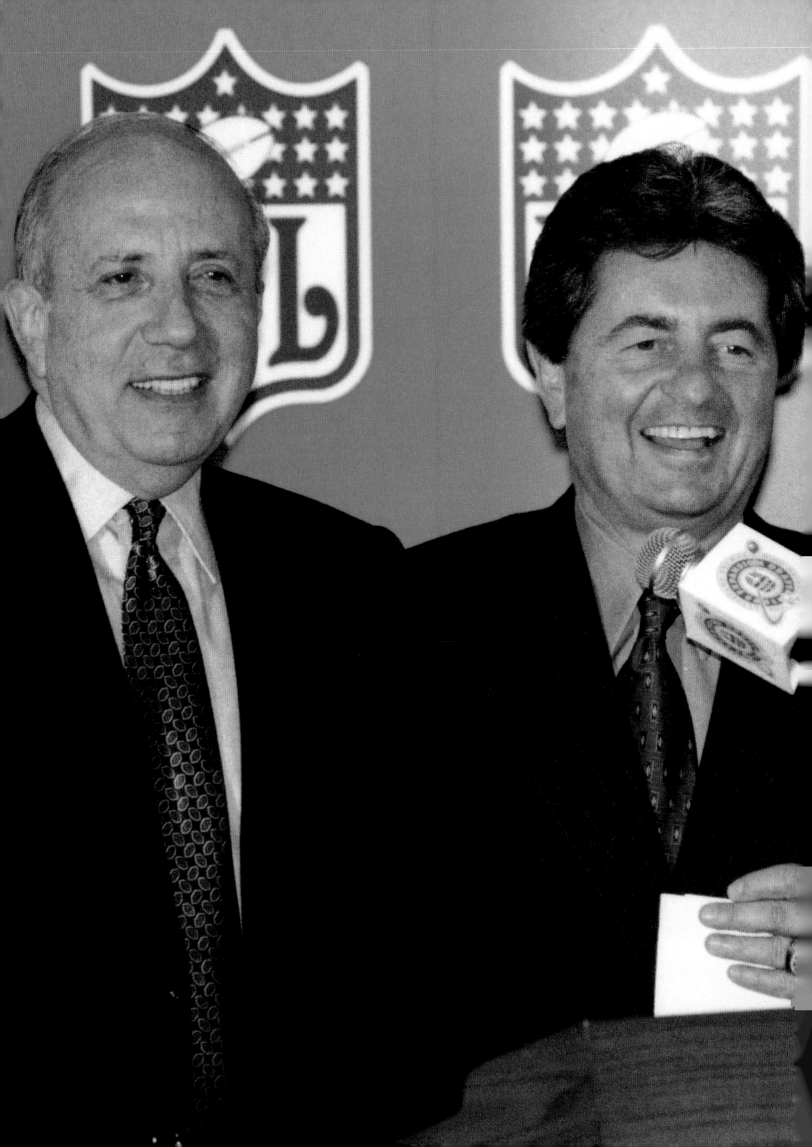

Al Lerner committed to building a tradition of success

BY STEVE HERRICK

Al Lerner and Carmen Policy at the NFL expansion draft in Canton on February 9, 1999, when the Browns selected 37 players.

In the case of the Browns' ownership groups, the last to enter the race ended up being the winner.

Rumors had flown for months during the first half of 1998 that Al Lerner, the successful Cleveland businessman, would form a group to make a bid for the expansion franchise that was to begin play in 1999. Lerner is chairman and chief executive officer of MBNA Corporation (NYSE), the largest independent bank lender through credit cards in the United States, with more than 20,000 employees worldwide including 1,800 in the greater Cleveland area. ➤

He is also Chairman and Chief Executive Officer of Town and Country Trust (NYSE; 17,000 residential apartments).

Despite the urging of Cleveland Mayor Michael White, Lerner stayed quiet as several other groups joined the race. But Lerner, who had given his support to White's mayoral candidacy, did have ties to the NFL and had a relationship with Commissioner Paul Tagliabue that dated to the 1970s. At that time Lerner hired Tagliabue, then a Washington lawyer, to defend his banking company in a court case. That began a friendship between the two men. As negotiations continued in 1996 between the NFL and the city to bring football back to Cleveland, Lerner used his connections with Tagliabue to help guarantee the city a team.

After the deal between the league and the city was finalized, White picked Lerner and other local executives to lead the sale of luxury suites for the new stadium. Lerner personally called members of the corporate community and encouraged them to buy a suite. He also leased two suites for MBNA.

Still, Lerner probably wouldn't have gotten involved if not for a phone call from San Francisco 49ers president Carmen Policy in July 1998. Their messages to each other during the conversation: Lerner wasn't going to bid for the team unless Policy joined his group. And Policy wasn't going to join any team but Lerner's.

"When Carmen called, that changed the equation," Lerner said. "Until then, there was no chance."

Hiring Policy to run the team represented the first step in Lerner's campaign to build a winning organization. "The highest probability of doing that was to get Carmen to lead the effort," Lerner said. "Once he became available, it gave Cleveland its best shot compared to any other possibility."

Policy helped build the San Francisco 49ers into an NFL power. During his tenure as president, the 49ers won six division titles and

"When Carmen called, that changed the equation," Lerner said. "Until then, there was no chance."

one Super Bowl. Policy's boyhood friend Eddie DeBartolo Jr. owned the 49ers, who had become the league's model franchise under their leadership of the Youngstown natives. However, a rift had developed between the two men by that summer. DeBartolo's legal problems forced him to step down and had thrown the 49ers' front office into chaos. Policy began looking at other opportunities around the league and asked Tagliabue about Lerner. The commissioner gave a ringing endorsement.

"He said he would be an excellent owner in the NFL," Policy said of his talk with Tagliabue.

Policy then called Lerner. The two met for the first time a few days later and the formation of the group was set in motion. Policy resigned from the 49ers on July 22. The following day Lerner and Policy announced their intentions to acquire the Browns. Their group was quickly endorsed by White and they became the immediate front-runners to win the race. The group's announcement came a week before the league would screen the ownership groups and about six weeks before the franchise was to be awarded.

The National Football League awarded the Cleveland franchise to Alfred Lerner and President and CEO Carmen Policy on September 8, 1998, with the formal transfer of ownership from the Browns Trust to Lerner and Policy occurring on October 23, 1998.

"We consider the ownership of the Cleveland Browns to represent a very serious responsibility. We will work very hard to make the people of Cleveland and northern Ohio proud of their football team," said Lerner. "It is very exciting and scary because the point is not just to bring football back to Cleveland. We will go out there on Sunday to win, not just to play."

Lerner is well known for his contributions to and leadership in Cleveland's health-care and educational communities as well as for numerous charitable actions that have made a major impact through-

Al Lerner on the field in Tampa before a 1999 preseason game against the Buccaneers.

out Cleveland. Lerner serves as president and trustee of the Cleveland Clinic Foundation where the Lerner Research Institute is working on new treatments for cancer, coronary artery disease and AIDS. At University Hospitals, where his wife Norma is a trustee, there is also the Lerner Tower, a 210-bed state-of-the-art hospital building.

Lerner, who served in the U.S. Marine Corps from 1955 to '57 (achieving the rank of first lieutenant), is vice chairman and trustee of Columbia University and also is a trustee at Case Western Reserve University and New York Presbyterian Hospital. He also is a director of the Marine Corps Law Enforcement Association. Norma Lerner is a trustee of the Musical Arts Association (which supports the Cleveland Orchestra).

Lerner was born in Brooklyn, New York, graduated from Brooklyn Technical High School in 1951 and obtained a B.A. from Columbia College in 1955. He and his wife, the former Norma Wolkoff, reside in Shaker Heights. They have two children and six grandchildren.

Carmen's Policy ensures success

Carmen Policy is president and chief executive officer of the Cleveland Browns. He is responsible for creating a football and front-office organization for the National Football League's newest franchise, while building on the Browns' rich history and legacy. Owner and Chairman Alfred Lerner named Policy a 10 percent equity partner upon being awarded the franchise on September 8, 1998

Heading into the 1999 season, Policy said winning games was not as important as building a winning foundation for the future. "I do not think it is important that we do amazingly well in terms of wins and losses," he said. "I think it is important that we play well, conduct ourselves professionally and that the chemistry of the team be solid and work well."

That said, Policy does have ambitious goals, and losing will not be acceptable for long. "We are here with a very simple mandate: build the best sports organization in America, make sure it lives here in Cleveland, and make sure it does very well," he said.

"I do not know when we could see ourselves in the Super Bowl," Policy said, "but if we are not there in five years, I will personally feel I have not accomplished a goal I set for myself before I even knew who the players, coaches and personnel people would be for this team."

Al Lerner, Chris Palmer and Carmen Policy outside the locker room in Canton after the Browns won the Hall of Fame Game in overtime against Dallas, 20-17, on August 9, 1999.

Policy earned a reputation as one of the preeminent executives in professional sports during eight years as president and chief executive officer of the San Francisco 49ers. Both *The Sporting News* and *Pro Football Weekly* named him NFL Executive of the Year in 1994, the latter award having been determined by a vote of NFL owners and executives. *The Sporting News* and *GQ* magazine have also named him as one of the most influential people in professional sports.

Known for his swift, decisive style, rapid grasp of complex issues and ability to solve problems adeptly, Policy played a key role in all five of the 49ers' Super Bowl-winning teams and helped shape the course for a 49ers organization that became widely viewed as the hallmark sports franchise of the 1980s and '90s.

While practicing law in his native Youngstown, Ohio, Policy served the 49ers' front office in 1983 as vice president and general counsel. Upon becoming executive vice president in 1989, he took on added responsibility for the team's front-office activities and represented the 49ers on league matters. He was promoted to president and chief executive officer in 1991, at which time he moved to the San Francisco Bay area.

One of Policy's biggest challenges came after the 1993 season, when he was given a mandate to build a championship team. Creatively applying the NFL's new salary cap rules, he retained key veterans and signed top-quality free agents and draft picks to create a team that responded by winning Super Bowl XXIX.

While with the 49ers, Policy was a member of the NFL Finance Committee and the Committee on Opportunities and Challenges.

An ardent believer in public service, Policy is on the Board of Directors of the Cleveland Clinic Foundation and he expects to maintain a high level of civic and charitable involvement in Cleveland, similar to the level of involvement he maintained in San Francisco. Those efforts earned him numerous honors, including the prestigious Silver Cable

"We are here with a very simple mandate: build the best sports organization in America, make sure it lives here in Cleveland, and make sure it does very well."

— CARMEN POLICY

During eight years as president and chief executive officer of the San Francisco 49ers, Carmen Policy became known as one of the best executives in professional sports.

Pittsburgh owner Dan
Rooney, NFL Commis-
sioner Paul Tagliabue, Al
Lerner and Carmen
Policy at a banquet at
Cleveland Browns
Stadium on September
11, 1999, the night before
the season opener.

Car Award from the San Francisco Convention and Visitors Bureau for contributions to the development of the city's business community. He also received The Mayor's Fiscal Advisory Committee Award in recognition of his managerial experience.

Policy graduated from Youngstown Ursuline High and is a 1963 graduate of Youngstown State University, which honored him as Alumnus of the Year in 1997. He earned his Juris Doctorate Degree from Georgetown University Law Center in 1966. While he was practicing law, he was listed in all of the existing editions of the highly respected publication *The Best Lawyers in America*. Inclusion in the publication is a significant honor since it is based on peer evaluation.

Policy has five children. James, a graduate of University of Notre Dame and of Ohio State University College of Medicine, completed his residency at Stanford University and is serving a fellowship in pediatric orthopedics in Portland, Oregon. Daniel, a Notre Dame and Hastings College of Law graduate, is associated with Morgan Stanley in New York City and Amsterdam. Edward, a Notre Dame and Stanford Law School graduate, is affiliated with the Cleveland law firm of Thompson Hine & Flory LLP. Kerry, a graduate of Miami University in Oxford, Ohio, received her MBA and Master's in Media Administration degrees from Syracuse University and is currently working for MBNA. Kathy is also a graduate of Notre Dame and will be graduating from Stanford Law School in June, 2000.

Policy is married to the former Gail Moretti. They make their home in Cleveland

How 49er Red turned into
Cleveland Brown

A TALE HOLLYWOOD COULD TURN INTO A SCRIPT

Carmen Policy's journey to Cleveland began when a phone call from a friend interrupted his vacation in Maui. The call had nothing to do with football, but it would eventually lead Policy to a historic rendezvous with Al Lerner in Manhattan. The meeting, which would last 15 hours, cemented a partnership that promises a glorious future for professional football in Cleveland. In a conversation with Back Home editor Tim Graham before the start of the 1999 season, Policy explained why he joined the Cleveland Browns and why he thinks the franchise possesses unlimited potential for greatness.

Q: With all the success you enjoyed with the San Francisco 49ers, you could have gone just about anywhere in the National Football League. Why did you choose the Cleveland Browns?

It all came together in a serendipitous fashion. I wasn't looking to go anywhere at the time. I was anticipating staying in San Francisco and trying to work my way through some difficult challenges and more or less wait out the storm. But I had been involved in the Cleveland expansion process as part of the NFL Finance Committee, so I had some idea as to what was transpiring and how exciting it could be, and what a wonderful opportunity was waiting there for

Opening Night against
Pittsburgh, September
12, 1999.

whoever it was that would get the franchise and
have the opportunity to put together an organization literally from scratch. Yet, although it was a
startup organization, it was unlike any other
expansion franchise that the history of sports had
ever seen. It may be an expansion team in its first
year, but it is really not an expansion franchise
because it has a history, tradition and existing fan

Al Lerner and
Carmen Policy.

base which I have always said but now have truly come to experience
as the best in all of professional sport. And when the situation
presented itself that caused me to talk to Al Lerner for the first time,
and actually the two of us began exploring this uncharted area kind
of hand in hand, it just started getting more and more exciting.

And then, almost in a whimsical way, I made a decision based
upon a meeting that took probably about 15 hours in the course of
one day, what was in fact the first time I had ever met this person
before who I had known as being one of the most successful busi-
nessmen in America. But again I was in a situation that was very
perplexing and I was ready to go into a new situation which could be
even more perplexing if I weren't associating myself with the right
person. And yet I think that Al Lerner being the type of person that
I heard he was and that he appeared to be in our meeting, coupled
with the phenomenal opportunity he was offering, just became too
enticing to pass up. And fortunately I can say I was wrong about my
initial impressions because it turned out to be much, much better
than I thought. And he turned out to be an even more wonderful
partner, influence and source of support than I could ever hope.

Q: So you were leaving for a positive rather than escaping a negative?

Precisely. And the story of how the action came together by way of a phone call, it's the material that Hollywood would make into a script.

Q: Can you talk about that scenario?

We were having some tough times in San Francisco. The organization was in turmoil because we were experiencing indirection as well as lack of direction relative to what was happening with the ownership group. And in the minds of most, Eddie DeBartolo was still the primary figure in terms of the 49ers from an ownership standpoint, and yet in fact based upon an arrangement made with the National Football League, the family corporation under the control of Marie Denise DeBartolo York was technically in charge. But it wasn't working that way. I was getting frustrated and concerned because I wasn't able to run the organization the way I had been able to. And I just didn't know where we were going. And the league didn't appear to be either able to or committed to resolving that situation in short order.

So I was on the beaches of Maui for the Fourth of July holiday weekend in 1998. My wife made mention of the fact that we had forgotten to bring something down from the room, and in a very dutiful way I was finally coerced into going up to the room to get what we had forgotten.

Q: What was it?

It was a book plus the 25-protection sunscreen. I was the one who wanted to walk down the beach and go up to the beach bar. A condition to taking the walk was the sunscreen. So I went up and there's the light blinking. So I call and my assistant, Faye Donovan, says Dennis Swanson called and he says it's a matter of great significance to you that you call him because it involves gainful employment for your daughter. Dennis was the president of ABC Sports, and when Disney took over he kind of gracefully exited and runs NBC's affiliate in Manhattan. And he had become a friend. My daughter had just finished her dual master's degree at Syracuse had worked for NBC for a summer, and Dennis was serving as a reference for her. When you hear one of your kids has a possibility of finally getting gainful employment, that takes priority over everything. So I called him and he told me my daughter had told him she wanted to start in a market like Atlanta or Cleveland, did not want to go to New York or Los Angeles and didn't think it would be right to come to San Francisco. In the process of trying to help her wind up in Cleveland he called Al Lerner, and Mr. Lerner indicated maybe she should get a real job instead of working for a TV station.

I say, "I can't have my daughter bother Al Lerner. I may have shaken his hand once at a game, but I don't recall meeting him."

And Dennis says, "By the way, Al Lerner started talking about football. I started telling him he's the right guy for the Cleveland Browns. But he's not going to get involved. Friends asked him to get involved, but he doesn't want to run anything. If the right guy came along maybe he would have been interested, but that hadn't been the case."

Dennis pushed me to call Al Lerner about the Cleveland thing. I thanked him for everything and went downstairs. By the way, I forgot the sunscreen and I had to go back up again.

My wife and I took a walk on the beach and I started telling her about this call. Her reaction in the first place was we have a life on the West Coast. She said, "I know you may not stay with 49ers, but we were thinking of doing something primarily in the Bay Area, if not maybe in L.A." But she said, "You've got to think about it. What's Mr. Lerner like?" I say, "Well, I don't know. I've just read about him and heard about him."

Then, finally, he said in his typical businesslike way, I guess it's time we put the foreplay aside and we have one of those physical meetings.

Q: So did you call?

I never called him. When I got home from Hawaii, Dennis Swanson called me. We were talking about personal stuff. We were partners with a racehorse that truly didn't deserve to be in a glue factory. And he said, "Did you call Al Lerner?" And he got on me a little bit and said it's a great thing. "Even if you're not interested you owe it to your daughter because that's a great company. So two days later I put a call in. And shortly after putting the call in I was able to reach Al Lerner and we started talking. And he never brought up the Browns. All we talked about was Kerry, my daughter, and what she wanted to do in life. And he says, "Dennis mentioned you might be interested in football and from what I've heard you'd be a natural. You'd be great. And looking at it from the perspective of the league, you're the type of owner that we need in this business."

And Lerner explained how he doesn't run things. He's not an operator, even at MBNA. He didn't say any more. And I say, "If you had the right person?" We started the minuet and that started a telephone romance. We talked for about 10 days. Then, finally, he said in his typical businesslike way, I guess it's time we put the foreplay aside and we have one of those physical meetings. So I made arrangements to fly to his Manhattan office, I think Monday the 20th of July. I also made arrangements to have dinner with the commissioner the Sunday night before. Sunday night I met with Paul Tagliabue and sought his counsel and I told him I was meeting with Al Lerner and told him it's really the right thing for the 49ers for me to leave.

I didn't know when, but soon. He wasn't very excited about it. He was excited about Al Lerner but he was very concerned about the 49ers, the situation with Eddie, with him and his sister, unrest in the organization and on top of it all the stadium issue. (San Francisco voters approved a new football stadium in 1997, but the project remained in limbo, causing the NFL to cancel plans for the 49ers to host the 2003 Super Bowl.) We all worked very hard and committed a lot of personal capital for that stadium, including the commissioner. He wasn't enthusiastic and didn't say, "Good luck, I'm with you." It's more like, "We've got to think this thing through." He was thinking more of the 49ers than he was the Cleveland Browns' expansion process, Al Lerner or Carmen Policy. But I understood that and I think that's part of what makes him a good commissioner. I didn't appreciate it necessarily at the time because I think I wanted a little more tender loving care than I was getting, and personal support. But upon reflection, I understood.

Q: So what was the meeting like?

I met Al Lerner first thing Monday morning. I'm really not intimidated by people and circumstances. But when I walked into his office on the 50th floor of this gorgeous building overlooking Central Park, my jaw dropped open. I was the kid from the farm coming to the big city. It has a panoramic view of Central Park. You could literally see every tree in Central Park. The East River and Hudson River. It's breathtaking.

There are masterpieces hanging on the wall. He comes out and he's gracious. We ate three meals together that day, two in his office and one at his home. We covered everything. How we grew up, how we went to school. What our goals in life were. How were our relationships with our parents? How did we view friends? What's your theory on how to build an organization? I've never experienced anything like that in my life.

I kept trying to look behind the façade of the person I was dealing with to see what was really there. I felt very uneasy in a sense because I sensed that what I saw was genuine and you don't want to trust that at first. You want to have your guard up. You want to be

The new Cleveland Browns Stadium
was designed with more than football
in mind. The stadium includes a number
of meeting rooms, lounges and reception
areas like this one overlooking downtown
Cleveland.

Finally, he said, "If you're willing to do it, I'm willing to do it. Are you willing to do it?"
I said, "You want an answer now?"

positioned so that you get the real flavor of what the person is all about and all the while the guard kept slipping and we interacted with each other in a very forthright fashion.

I had to take off before midnight if I was going to leave New York that night. Finally, he said, "If you're willing to do it, I'm willing to do it. Are you willing to do it?"

I said, "You want an answer now?"

And he said, "If you're not at a point where you're ready to give an answer now, you probably shouldn't do it. This is something you really have to want to do. You're the type of man who's used to making decisions. So you don't need a lot of time to make those decisions."

And I said, "Yes, I want to do it."

Q: Where were you then?

At his home on Fifth Avenue. It's after midnight. And at 12:25 a.m. We shook hands. Then I flew over to Youngstown to meet Denise DeBartolo York on Tuesday. She was shocked. And I think at first she counted on me to be there to get everyone through it. But I honestly felt that my leaving would be part of the solution and that my staying might contribute to the problems. After she got over the first wave of reaction, she was very supportive. "I've been working on trying to get you a new contract," she said. "But if this is what you really want to do . . ."

Q: Then what?

I went out to the Youngstown airport. Al Lerner flew in to meet me. He picked me up and we went to Cleveland. We went to his house and faced the biggest obstacle to moving forward with the Cleveland Browns expansion process. That was Norma Lerner. She was not for this at all. As far as she's concerned her husband has been a private person. His biggest exposure was being honored by Columbia University for contributions, support and money. That would be the most he'd venture out because he's a very serious businessman who's not a public person. And all of a sudden he's going to own a football team in his hometown after all of the publicity and notoriety that had been attached to the Cleveland Browns. When we got there he said, "By the way, I haven't sold Norma on this yet."

And then I met her and she's just wonderful. And she embraced me and ultimately, because I think she sensed that this was something that Al really wanted to do, she embraced the idea. I don't think she was for it. But she went along with it.

The mayor came over that night. Mayor White was really ebullient. He was gregarious, animated. He says, "This is the best news since we got the word from the league that we were going to get a team." He was going to come out and support us. We thought he shouldn't because it might be damaging to him politically, because there were some very prominent Clevelanders in a competing group.

He said, "This isn't a matter of selecting personalities. It's a matter of my going with the group that I think has the best chance of putting the best organization together and a winning team on the field. And I've got so much of myself invested in the Cleveland Browns and the building of that stadium that I can't afford to have the matter turned over to people that I don't think can necessarily get the job done. Al Lerner, I know you can get it done." And that's how we started.

That night I get back on his plane. When I'm in the air I call our PR department with the 49ers and we set up a news conference at 10:30 at the San Francisco airport the next morning. We finish at 12. Then I get back on the airplane and fly back to Cleveland. And Al Lerner and I made our announcement on Thursday.

Q: At the Hall of Fame Game in Canton, you said, "We're not an expansion team. We're the Cleveland Browns." Could you elaborate on what you meant?

Typically expansion teams are entities that are created and planted for the first time in a community, and their history begins with their launch. Then they go from there. And people who become their fan base are either interested in sports as a whole, or community-minded or looking for a new event to identify with or enjoy. There is no history. The Cleveland Browns, on the other hand, have one of the most storied and fascinating histories and backgrounds of any team in the NFL. We have heroes. We even have villains. And this community is so wedded to the concept of the Browns that is really right up there with family and religion. Part of it's where we are. We're right here in the birthplace of pro football, just 60 miles away in Canton, Ohio.

My wife is a perfect example of what the Browns mean to this area. She remembers as a girl, you get up on Sunday, you go to Mass with Mom and Dad. You stop at the bakery on the way home and buy two or three loaves of bread. You have the main meal of the day on Sunday around noon. You clean up the dishes, you sit down and you watch the Browns. Family, church, Browns. And it all came together with me. I was telling her about how I can't believe the community. I can't believe the enthusiasm, commitment, excitement, how deep it runs, with women as well as men. And with children. And then she told me that story and she framed it for me. What we have here is no expansion franchise per se. You just have a situation where there was a hiatus in the operation of the Cleveland Browns, so they can reorganize, build a new stadium, get their act together and come back stronger than ever. And that's how I believe the fans are viewing it today. And that's what I feel. I think this organization now, for a variety of reasons, is one of the strongest in all of football, even though our team is by far the newest.

The Office Max Club
Lounge inside Cleveland
Browns Stadium.

Q: As you look to the future, what do you see?

A lot of hard work and a boundless amount of optimism. Everyone is viewing our horizons as being unlimited. People who work here, they feel there's no ceiling. Everyone can grow and develop and set records. Limited only by ourselves and whatever limitations that might be on our talent and energy. The fans could not be better. What you're seeing from our fans is not the normal hype that comes with the attachment to the new kid on the block. They're very astute when it comes to pro football. They understand the game. They understand the practical aspects of running this kind of organization. They respect good management as well as great play on the field. And they're supporting us. As long as we do our job, as long as we are continually motivated to put a winner on the field, I think that there'd be no greater environment than the Cleveland Browns organization within which to work in all of professional football. Plus, when you have every resource you could want available to you with the only requirement being use it wisely — that's it, don't waste it, use it wisely, and it's there — you just can't ask for anything more.

We have a limit on excuses for losing. There are no excuses here. I'm not talking about in 1999. I'm talking about within a reasonable period of time, shame on us if we're not a real contender for the Super Bowl. Because should we not reach that point, it's our shortcomings, our individual shortcomings. We've got the fan base, we've got phenomenal ownership who's committed in a responsible way to doing what's right whether it relates to the field or the community. We have some smart people working here who are experienced. If we keep our heads on our shoulders and screwed on right I think the probabilities are we're going to be there.

So I was really a Doubting Thomas. I kept looking for everything wrong, because there had to be a lot more wrong with this and it couldn't be this nice.

Q: The new Cleveland Browns Stadium is awesome. What went through your mind the first time you saw it?

Back in September of 1998, after we had been awarded the franchise, my initial reaction was I can't believe that this facility, under the direction of a municipality without the supervision of ownership, could be this nice. So I was always looking for the downside of things because I just couldn't give local government the credit that you'd have to give.

So I was really a Doubting Thomas. I kept looking for everything wrong, because there had to be a lot more wrong with this and it couldn't be this nice.

Part of the reason was that Al Lerner quietly upgraded a lot of the items. He put his money on the table quietly to make sure that things were done right and the best.

It came together and here we are having opened the stadium against Minnesota, and it's phenomenal. The people who were there, including architects, contend that it's probably, although they hate to say it, it's probably the best in the NFL. When you look at those openings in the stands, I knew I liked it. I knew it was different. But I didn't realize how much I liked it. Because it brings the outside in when you're inside, and it brings you into it when you're outside.

Q: What's the best part?

Intimacy. That's the one word I use to characterize the greatest accomplishment of the Cleveland Browns Stadium. The feeling of intimacy with the field. Intimacy is the key to that whole thing.

Q: What's the most important decision you've made since joining the Browns?

Probably the hiring of Chris Palmer. And that was a decision that was made in conjunction with Al Lerner and Dwight Clark. In my mind it was always a foregone conclusion that if I came here I wanted Dwight Clark to be the director of football operations. So I don't view that as decision made after I got here. Once here, there's no question that hiring Chris Palmer became the most important decision that the three of us would be making in terms of getting this organization off to the right start.

Q: Why did you choose Palmer?

He wasn't high on my list originally. Of course, I had never met him. But he shot right to the top and shared a spot at the top with one or two others after the first interview. It was because he struck me as a man loaded with sincerity and credibility. His background, in the pros, in the college ranks and even in the ranks more junior than college, indicated that he was a great teacher. He loved the game. I think he'd coach for nothing if he thought his family would be taken care of, and that was the only way he could coach. I really think he loves the game and coaching that much. Plus, he seemed to be so balanced as a human being and as a professional. When you think about what you needed in place here in this organization at this time in its history, as I look back I'm not sure there's another person alive in America today who fits that profile of head coach of the Cleveland Browns during their commemorative season and thereafter to build this team again from the grassroots up. I don't think there's anybody who could fit the bill better.

Chris Palmer, whose reputation as a great teacher helped him win the Browns' coaching job, counsels rookie Ronnie Powell after he fumbled a kickoff return in the Opening Night loss to Pittsburgh.

Q: Is there anything you'd do differently?

I would have tried to have been better organized. Even if it required having a temporary staff. Because I have found there were things I didn't address that I had traditionally addressed in every position I've ever had, whether it was in football or outside football. Such as try to return calls. I fell so far behind that the only way I could avoid the distraction and the pangs of guilt that I had stacks of messages that were measured in half-a-foot categories was to throw them all away. Never before in my life, not as a lawyer, not as a businessman, not as an NFL executive, never have I done that. But I literally couldn't get on with doing the stuff I had to do with those stacks facing me unless I threw them all away. And that is a terribly irresponsible way of addressing situations but it was the only way I could address it and move forward.

I didn't have a chance to see people who wanted to sit down with me. I think I hurt some feelings that I otherwise would not want to hurt. I wasn't able to deal with the existing alumni as well as I would have liked to, and I was constantly putting that on the back burner because I knew what had to be done in such short order, to get this organization up and running and have the team on the field and the stadium completed. I don't know if there was something I could have done to pay more attention to some of those details that were not on the very, very front end of our priority list.

And I probably should have been a little more considerate of my wife. I probably did not show her the kind of appreciation that she deserved for all that she went through and the way she handled the transition. But other than that, no regrets. Part of that is because Al Lerner was so supportive through the whole process. He was there when I needed him. He felt if being around would cause us to pay too much attention to him, he wouldn't show up intentionally. Money never was a problem. When an issue came up that was financially connected, if in my mind I could justify it, I never gave it a second thought. And again, that's because of the man that started this and his commitment to doing not only the right thing, but whatever is necessary to build the best. Do you realize what a luxury that is?

I don't think we could have gotten it done, in the way we got it done, with the net result being what we perceive it to be, without Al Lerner. And that goes right back to what you've heard every time an evaluation of a sports franchise becomes the subject of discussion. It starts at the top. And I could see it form the day I met him. You could see it in everything he does. Without the proper ownership, organizations don't have a shot, especially in pro sports. They can get lucky, and they'll get that spike in the chart, but I predict that that they can't maintain it for very long and then they'll experience a spike in the other direction, and that's why this league is so intent on making sure we get the type of owner that's quality.

Q: There's an eight-word question on the mind of every Browns fan. When are we going to the Super Bowl?

Every Browns fan, including Al Lerner. He asks me that now and then. I know what it's like to get to the Super Bowl. I've been there with an organization that's been successful in playing in the big game five times, and, thank God, winning five times. And even in the years where you had everything going for you and probably had somehow, some way put the best team in football together, you needed luck to still make it. Because I look back and if just a few things had happened another way, notwithstanding all the right things you did, you probably wouldn't have made it. It's so difficult to get there that to predict with any degree of authority a time frame within which you'll make it is foolhardy.

Browns fans lived up to their reputation as second to none in enthusiasm throughout a challenging 1999 season.

"This is never going to happen again. There's never going to be another expansion team that has a history. There's never going to be another situation like this."

CHRIS PALMER

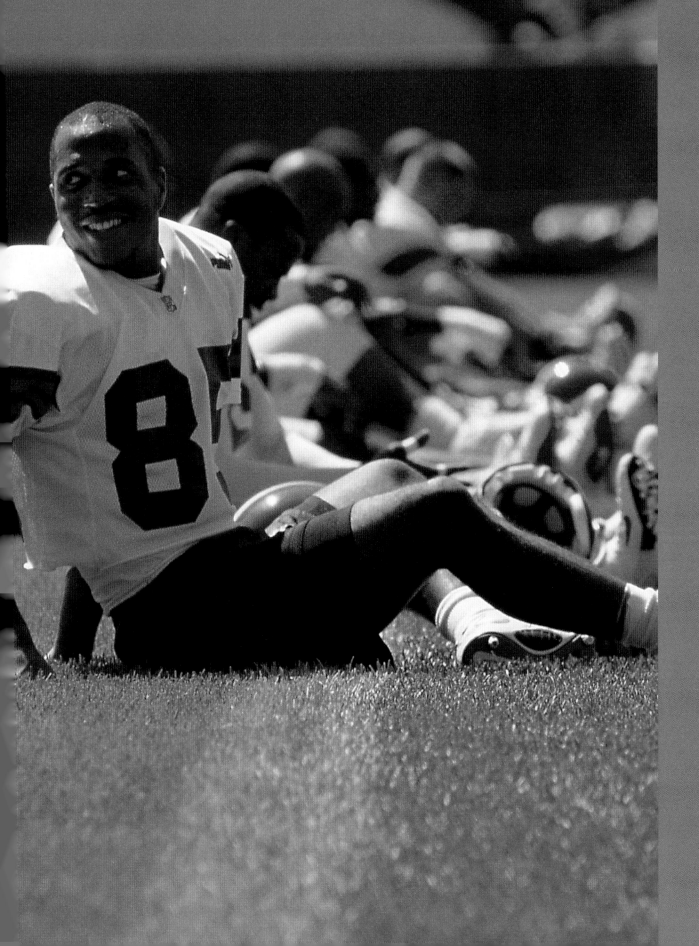

BUILDING A WINNING FOUNDATION

The only man in America for the job

BY STEVE HERRICK

o

Chris Palmer wants everyone to know about the history of the Cleveland Browns. That's why he showed his players on the expansion team a video of the Browns' history the night before their first training camp opened, in July 1999. Palmer knows all about the franchise's rich tradition. He wanted to make sure everyone involved with the new Browns knew all about it too.

As coach of the new Browns, Palmer understands the significance of the team's return to the NFL. ➤

"All I am is the caretaker for the Cleveland Browns. The tradition and pride of the Browns is something we will cherish and build on."

"This is never going to happen again," he said. "There's never going to be another expansion team that has a history. There's never going to be another situation like this."

Palmer knows what Browns fans went through in the three years without football, after the original franchise moved to Baltimore following the 1995 season.

"My dad was a Brooklyn Dodgers fan, so I know how he felt when the Dodgers left for Los Angeles in the '50s," said Palmer. "The Cleveland Browns coming back would be like the Brooklyn Dodgers coming back."

Palmer knows football and he knows what it means in Cleveland.

"I knew the passion people have for this team," he said. "The fan base and the love of football is unique. It's what I want. All I am is the caretaker for the Cleveland Browns. To me, it's the fans who own the team. It's the fans it means so much to. The tradition and pride of the Browns is something we will cherish and build on."

Palmer was the offensive coordinator of the Jacksonville Jaguars for two seasons before being hired by the Browns on January 21, 1999. Counting college, the Canadian Football League, the United States Football League and the NFL, he had 27 years of coaching experience when the Browns came calling.

"In every job, there are negatives, but I couldn't find a single one here," he said.

Over his nine years as an NFL assistant, Palmer was recognized as one of the top offensive minds in the game.

"The favorite thing I do is teach," he said.

While in Jacksonville, Palmer helped mold Mark Brunell into one of the top quarterbacks in the league. Prior to joining the Jaguars, he spent four seasons in New England and developed quarterback Drew Bledsoe into a star. Browns owner Al Lerner and president and chief operating officer Carmen Policy are counting on him to do the same

The coach with his
prized pupil.

thing with franchise quarterback Tim Couch, the No. 1 pick in the 1999 draft.

Everyone who comes into contact with Palmer talks about what a nice guy he is. And he looks like a nice guy. With his balding head and glasses, Palmer looks like the friendly neighbor with whom you would spend hours shooting the breeze.

"We hired a really good guy," said Policy. "He's a real person."

Palmer was one of several assistant coaches from around the NFL to interview for the head coaching job. He impressed Lerner, Policy and Dwight Clark right away.

"We went out of the room (during the interview) and huddled," said Lerner. "We all agreed this guy was so close to what we wanted."

Palmer knows all about his nice-guy image. And he's not completely happy with it.

"I think one of the concerns about me was that I was too nice of a guy to be a head coach," he said. "I'm not out to be a bad guy, but I have standards. I tell the players, here is the line. If you don't cross the line, we'll never have a problem."

It didn't take Browns players long to discover what happens when that line gets crossed. Any

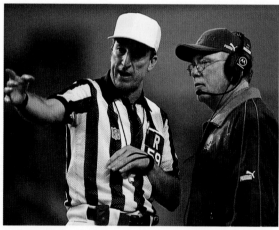

ABOVE AND RIGHT: Palmer normally remained calm even when calls went the other way.

player who came to training camp overweight felt the wrath of Palmer, who admits he could lose a few pounds himself.

"There's only going to be one fat guy around here, and it's me," said the coach.

The players also learned early on the coach doesn't miss a thing in practice. The quiet of one early-morning session in training camp was disrupted by an angry Palmer after the offense didn't get out of the huddle quickly enough.

"Why can't we get up there quicker?" he yelled. "We gotta get to the line faster than that! Let's go!"

"There's only going to be one fat guy around here, and it's me,"

When the same thing happened the very next play, Palmer erupted again and all movement around him stopped.

"We're going to have to do it quicker than that when it matters!" he yelled. "We can't be doing that in a game!"

For someone who looks like such a nice guy, Palmer's voice has a certain kick to it. You could be one yard or 50 yards away, and you'll hear it.

"His voice echoes," said linebacker Jamir Miller. "It seems like we've got a canyon wall out there."

As the Browns kickers struggled throughout that first summer, Palmer quickly lost patience. And he didn't want to hear any excuses.

"It's not like a guy has to spend three years in placekicking purgatory," said Palmer. "He can either kick here or he can't."

The players usually get the message. Those who don't aren't around very long.

"He can get pretty sarcastic," said quarterback Ty Detmer. "When he does that, you know he's not very happy."

"Coach doesn't mess around," said offensive lineman Jim Pyne. "When you're with him one-on-one, he's a pretty good guy. When he's on the field, he'll get on everybody. He'll yell at us. He'll yell at his assistant coaches. He'll even yell at the water boys."

Palmer wants this method to have a point.

"I don't yell just to yell," he said. "There is a reason for it. I'm an up-front guy. If something bothers me, I don't let it stew. I let it out."

"That's good," said Miller. "We know what he's thinking."

"You don't feel he's playing games," said Policy. "Although he's got a pretty even temperament, you also get the impression you better not play games with him. He's not going to tolerate it."

That's why the Browns believe the future of a franchise with such a storied tradition is in good hands.

Carmen's First Catch

Carmen Policy knew even before taking the helm of the Cleveland Browns that he wanted Dwight Clark to come with him. Clark, best known for making "the catch" against the Dallas Cowboys to win the 1981 NFC Championship and send the San Francisco 49ers to their first Super Bowl, is vice president and director of football operations for the Browns.

Clark is responsible for all aspects of the Browns' football operations, including managing and implementing the organizational structure of the department. He oversees all aspects of professional and college personnel, including contract negotiations and salary-cap considerations. One of his most important responsibilities is to work closely and in direct contact with the head coach on all matters affecting the team.

Before joining the Browns, Clark spent 19 seasons with the 49ers, nine as a player followed by 10 in the front office. During his last four he served as vice president/director of football operations. In that capacity, he was responsible for scouting, player personnel, contract negotiations, salary-cap management and the team's training camp. Previously he served as coordinator of football operations and player personnel, executive administrative assistant and marketing consultant. He was a part of all five of the 49ers' Super Bowl wins, as a player in Super Bowls XVI and XIX, and in XXIII, XXIV and

"It was always a foregone conclusion that if I came here I wanted Dwight Clark to be the director of football operations."

—CARMEN POLICY

XXXIX as a front-office executive. He ended his playing career as one of the 49ers' most popular players ever and at the time was the club's all-time leading receiver with 506 catches, 6,750 receiving yards and 48 touchdowns.

Clark enjoys a close relationship with Policy. "In my mind," Policy said, "it was always a foregone conclusion that if I came here I wanted Dwight Clark to be the director of football operations."

A native of Kinston, North Carolina, Clark majored in secondary education (history) at Clemson. He and his wife, Ashley, have three children.

The catch, which defeated the Cowboys in the 1981 NFC championship game and sent the 49ers to their first Super Bowl, remains one of the most memorable moments in NFL history.

How the Browns **were built**

O f the 53 Browns on the roster at the start of the 1999 season, 24 were signed as free agents, 14 were veteran players selected in the expansion draft, nine were selected in the collegiate draft and six were acquired through trades or waivers.

Free Agents

Derrick Alexander, Defensive End, Minnesota
Jerry Ball, Defensive Tackle, Minnesota
Lomas Brown, Offensive Tackle, Arizona
Orlando Brown, Offensive Tackle, Baltimore
Mark Campbell, Tight End
Ryan Collins, Tight End
Phil Dawson, Kicker
Corey Fuller, Defensive Back, Minnesota
Chris Gardocki, Punter, Indianapolis
Darrius Holland, Defensive Tackle, Detroit
John Jurkovic, Defensive Tackle, Jacksonville
Terry Kirby, Running Back, San Francisco
Ryan Kuehl, Defensive Tackle
Jamie Martin, Quarterback
Ryan McNeil, Cornerback, St. Louis
Arnold Miller, Defensive End

Jamir Miller, Linebacker, Arizona

Marquez Pope, Defensive Back, San Francisco

Ronnie Powell, Wide Receiver

Jeermaine Ross, Wide Receiver

Leslie Shepherd, Wide Receiver, Washington

John Thierry, Linebacker, Chicago

Dave Wohlabaugh, Center, New England

Steve Zahursky, Guard

ABOVE: Scott Rehberg came from the New England Patriots in the expansion draft.

RIGHT: Ty Detmer and Tim Couch.

Expansion Draft

Orlando Bobo, Guard, Minnesota

Jim Bundren, Center, New York Jets

Marlon Forbes, Defensive Back, Chicago

Darmon Gibson, Wide Receiver, Cincinnati

Ray Jackson, Defensive Back, Buffalo

Lenoy Jones, Linebacker, Tennessee

Antonio Langham, Defensive Back, San Francisco

Hurvin McCormack, Defensive Tackle, Dallas

Tim McTyer, Defensive Back, Philadelphia

Jim Pyne, Guard, Detroit

Scott Rehberg, Guard, New England

Tarek Saleh, Fullback, Carolina

Mike Thompson, Defensive Tackle, Cincinnati

James Williams, Linebacker, San Francisco

Collegiate Draft

Tim Couch, Quarterback, Kentucky

Kevin Johnson, Wide Receiver, Syracuse

Rahim Abdullah, Linebacker, Clemson

Daylon McCutcheon, Cornerback, Southern California

Marquis Smith, Safety, California

Wali Rainer, Linebacker, Virginia

Mark Campbell, Irv Smith
and Ty Detmer.

Darrin Chiaverini, Wide Receiver, Colorado
Marcus Spriggs, Defensive Tackle, Troy State
Kendall Ogle, Linebacker, Maryland

Trades and Waivers
Roy Barker, Defensive End, San Francisco
Alex Bernstein, Guard, New York Jets
Ty Detmer, Quarterback, San Francisco
Marc Edwards, Fullback, San Francisco
Sedrick Shaw, Running Back, New England
Irv Smith, Tight End, San Francisco

New Browns Who Were Old Browns
Three members of the new Browns played for the team before it moved
to Baltimore after the 1995 season:
Jerry Ball, Right Defensive Tackle, 1993
Orlando Brown, Offensive Tackle, 1993-1995
Antonio Langham, Defensive Back, 1994-1995

Browns Who Were 49ers
In addition to President and CEO Carmen Policy and Vice President
and Director of Football Operations Dwight Clark, nine players on
the roster at the start of the 199 season had ties to the 49ers in 1998:
Roy Barker, Defensive Lineman
Ty Detmer, Quarterback
Bill Duff, Defensive Lineman
Marc Edwards, Running Back
Terry Kirby, Running Back
Antonio Langham, Defensive Back
Marquez Pope, Defensive Back
Irv Smith, Tight End
James Williams, Linebacker

Couch's work ethic impresses his coach and teammates

BY STEVE HERRICK

The education of Tim Couch as an NFL quarterback began on April 17, 1999.

No, he didn't learn anything about X's and O's or picking up a blitz package. That's the day the Browns made him the first pick in the NFL draft. Both sides are confident that day will be the first chapter in what will be a long career for the Couch, who set just about every record imaginable at the University of Kentucky.

But that's not all Couch remembers from draft day. Picking after the Browns, the Philadelphia Eagles took another quarterback, Syracuse's Donovan McNabb. Philadelphia fans, jammed into the draft headquarters in New York City, almost booed McNabb out of the building because they wanted the Eagles to take running back Ricky Williams.

The irony wasn't lost on Couch. As he was whisked away to board a plane for a warm welcome in Cleveland, he thought about McNabb's reception and how easily that could have happened to him.

Call it his first lesson in the NFL.

"I really lucked out there," Couch said of winding up in Cleveland. "The fans here know football and I think they understand what I'm going through."

"Tim is very competitive. He won't give an inch."

— CHRIS PALMER

Couch may have been only 22 during his rookie season, but he displayed maturity beyond his years and seemed to know what he needed to do to be successful.

"I have enough talent to play," said Couch. "I've proven that. What's going to make me successful is being the hardest-working guy on the team."

Browns coach Chris Palmer is one of the most respected offensive minds in football. He knows quarterbacks and thinks Couch has the potential to be one of the best. But that's not what impresses Palmer the most.

"He's a football guy," said Palmer. "He's like Chris Spielman. He's the first one in and the last one to go. His work ethic is excellent."

Palmer remembers an incident that happened a few days before camp began. On an off-day for the players, Couch told Palmer he wanted to do some film work with the coach.

"I told him to go home and take a nap," said Palmer. "I told him to take a few hours off. I told him if he wanted to do some work later to give me a call."

Sure enough, Palmer's phone rang a few hours later and the two ended up looking at tape through the afternoon and evening.

On one occasion early in camp, quarterback coach John Hufnagel was making his nightly bed check. He found Couch and roommate Mike Cook, another rookie quarterback, studying their playbooks and diagramming plays.

Many rookies sign endorsements for commercials and have their faces all over local television. Couch surely could have cashed in on a lot of opportunities, but other than having his picture on some advertisements around the new Cleveland Browns Stadium, he declined.

The Browns opened training camp at their headquarters in Berea with four quarterbacks, Mike Cook, Tim Couch, John Dutton and Ty Detmer.

Tim Couch was a target
for autograph seekers
from the first day of
practice.

"Sometimes when a rookie hits the big money, it goes to his head, but that hasn't happened to him," said running back Terry Kirby. "You can tell he's serious about wanting to be a great player."

"That's not what I'm here for," said Couch. "I'm here to learn, play football and help this team win."

"I know some people offered him the chance to have a radio show," said Palmer. "He told me he didn't want to do it. I told him that was a great idea."

"Sometimes when a rookie hits the big money, it goes to his head, but that hasn't happened to him," said running back Terry Kirby. "You can tell he's serious about wanting to be a great player."

"Tim works hard," said Spielman. "He's fit in very well. Some rookies aren't like that."

Couch showed his maturity when he changed a play at the line of scrimmage in the first series of his first preseason game.

"Most rookie quarterbacks don't have the guts to make a change like that," said one veteran defensive player. "He did it the first time he was on the field. The kid is a natural."

People often wonder how young players, especially those who come into the league with Couch's hype, will respond to pressure. Couch showed he can handle pressure even before the draft. After an unimpressive workout in front of the Browns and several other NFL teams on March 11, Couch fell behind Oregon quarterback Akili Smith on Cleveland's draft board. Whispers about his lack of arm strength flew and many thought the Browns would be better off going in another direction with the No. 1 pick.

The Browns decided to take another look at Couch. A couple of weeks before the draft, Palmer and a large Browns contingent flew to Lexington for a make-or-break workout for Couch. In a grueling session, Palmer had Couch throw 115 passes. The quarterback passed with flying colors.

"I was trying to make him quit, but he wouldn't," said Palmer. "He kept coming and coming. He would have stayed another hour if I wanted him to."

"I started to get tired about halfway through," said Couch. "I could tell it wasn't going to end. I gritted my teeth and got fired up."

Palmer quickly learned about Couch's intensity.

"Tim is very competitive," said Palmer. "He won't give an inch."

Being the top pick in the draft and the central figure for an expansion franchise is a long way from Couch's hometown of Hyden, a small Kentucky town with a population of 350. After a stellar high school career, he was one of the most heavily recruited quarterbacks in the country, but chose to stay in his home state.

Even though he's 6-foot-4 and 227 pounds, Couch is a good athlete. He started for his high school football team in the ninth grade. He was such a good basketball player that former Kentucky coach Rick Pitino asked him to play for the Wildcats.

Despite staying at Kentucky for only three years, Couch shattered the school's passing records, throwing for 8,835 yards and 74 touchdowns. And he relied on improvisation for most of it.

"We didn't have a playbook at Kentucky," said Couch. "We kind of played sandlot ball. Coach [Hal] Mumme drew up half the plays in the dirt on the sidelines."

Mumme's game plan usually consisted of 15 to 20 plays. Palmer, meanwhile, has a playbook the size of many city phone directories. The Browns' playbook is at least six inches thick and contains more than 100 passing plays.

"Learning is part of the NFL," said Couch. "That's good for me. The more I learn, the better I'll be."

The Browns think Couch will learn. And in time be the cornerstone of the franchise.

"Tim Couch has always been the guy who's rallied the troops," said Vice President and Director of Football Operations Dwight Clark. "He's always been the leader. He set records in high school and college. We expect him to try to set records here."

Even veteran players
were impressed with the
rookie's poise and
confidence.

"Tim Couch has always been the leader. He set records in high school and college. We expect him to try to set records here."

DWIGHT CLARK

The first casualty:
A proud symbol of the new Browns

BY STEVE HERRICK

How did Chris Spielman start his last day as a professional football player?

No, he wasn't in an easy chair or preparing a retirement speech. Spielman began that day the same way he approached his entire career, from his days as a high school player in Massillon to his days at Ohio State to his days as a pro.

When Browns coach Chris Palmer walked into the team's training facility the morning of August 30, 1999, he heard some noise in the weight room. The fact that it was 6:30 a.m., an hour most professional athletes don't even know exists, made the commotion seem a little odd.

So Palmer investigated. There was Spielman, who had grudgingly come to the conclusion the day before that his career was over, lifting weights and taped as if he was getting ready to suit up for that day's practice.

Eight hours later, Spielman held a press conference. Yes, the career that made him a legend in the annals of Ohio football — a career that landed him on the cover of a Wheaties box when he was in high school — was indeed over. But the words retirement and quitting never came out of Spielman's mouth.

"We're all football warriors," he said. "Being that, you have to accept your mortality as a player. It is important for me to let everyone

Chris Spielman was unable to move for about 15 seconds after the last hit of his career, in a preseason game at home against Chicago, August 28, 1999.

"Some people asked me how I could take last year off to take care of my wife. What kind of a man would I be if I didn't?"

know I'm not quitting. I would never quit. I've never quit anything in my life. Surrender is not in my vocabulary." Spielman told his teammates of his decision earlier in the day. Again, those two nasty words were never mentioned.

"He told the team how fortunate they were to be in the National Football League," said Palmer. "He told them how fortunate he was to be a husband and a father and to have played in the NFL."

"Spielman's comeback had been among the most emotionally stirring parts of the Browns' return to the NFL. The hard-hitting linebacker injured his neck while playing for the Buffalo Bills during the 1997 season, and he needed surgery to fuse two vertebrae. While he was cleared medically to play in 1998, Spielman chose to sit out the season to be with his family as his wife, Stefanie, battled breast cancer.

The decision showed people another side of Spielman, who was an All-America twice at Ohio State and made four Pro Bowls after being drafted by the Detroit Lions in 1988.

Yes, he had always been consumed by football. This was a man who turned on the air-conditioner full blast the night before games in cold weather so he could get used to the conditions. Football people preach patience when it comes to building an expansion team. Not Spielman. A few days before camp opened, Browns vice president and director of football operations Dwight Clark said in a newspaper interview he didn't want to set unrealistic goals for the team in its first year. After reading the quotes, a furious Spielman stormed into the team's training complex and shouted, "Am I wasting my time here?"

Still, taking the year off was an easy decision.

"I'm a husband and a father first," he said. "Some people asked me how I could take last year off to take care of my wife. What kind of a man would I be if I didn't?"

After doctors declared Stefanie cancer-free, in January of 1999, the Browns acquired him from Buffalo a month later. All eyes in train-

Spielman warms up
before his final game.

ing camp were on Spielman, who got a scare on the first day when he collided violently with fullback Tarek Saleh. The blow sent Spielman to the hospital, but test results showed his neck had gotten stronger since the surgery.

Spielman and the Browns were confident he would be able to play, but those hopes ended on August 28, in the team's fourth preseason game. After a helmet-to-helmet hit with Chicago Bears center Casey Wiegmann, Spielman went down and couldn't get up.

"I laid on the field and I could not move arms, legs, anything," he said. "That lasted 10 or 15 seconds."

Spielman finally got to his feet and was helped off the field by team doctors and trainers. He walked to the locker room, tossing some of his equipment to young fans, and was taken to a hospital for more tests.

Spielman was taken to the hospital for tests after he was helped off the field.

The injury took the joy out of the Browns' 35-24 victory, their first win in their new stadium. Palmer, visibly concerned, talked to Spielman at 1 the next morning.

"He apologized to me for letting me down," said Palmer. "That was the only time I got upset with him in our seven months of being together. I said, 'You didn't let me down one bit.'"

Even though team doctors and specialists told Spielman he should retire, he still wanted to play. After talking with Palmer, Browns president Carmen Policy and Stefanie, Spielman reluctantly agreed it was over.

"You go through a lot of emotions," he said. "You're trained to feel you're invincible. When you go out on the field, you have to feel that way. I would love to keep playing, but I can't jeopardize my arms and my legs."

Spielman was the heart and soul of every team he played on.

"For me, as a Northeast Ohio kid, to play his last game on the Cleveland Browns field in front of Cleveland Browns fans in a Cleveland Browns helmet," he said, "I couldn't write it any better."

"The two things I'm most proud of as a player — my effort level and my toughness were never in question," he said. "They were never questioned by anyone at anytime from Pee Wee football to pro football. I'll hang my hat on that."

"Stefanie and Chris are a great story in themselves," said Policy. "I think their story and the type of people they are personify the spirit of the Cleveland Browns and the people of Cleveland. I couldn't imagine two finer people to be associated with that tell the story of what the Browns someday hope to be."

For Palmer, coaching Spielman was a pleasure.

"He's one of a kind," Palmer said. "He's a guy that owes everything to football. He's a guy that respects the game, has a passion for the game. His family is in football, he probably grew up with a football on the kitchen table. If there were more guys like that, coaching would be very easy."

As his career ended a few weeks before his 34th birthday, Spielman wasn't sure what his future held. Browns owner Al Lerner asked him to consider a job with the sports marketing division of MBNA, the credit card company Lerner owns. Palmer offered him a position as an assistant-linebacker coach with the Browns. Spielman mentioned he'd like to be the head coach at Ohio State someday. For the 1999 season he worked as a television commentator for Fox Sports.

Spielman knows some viewed his premature retirement with sadness, but he would have none of that.

"I leave with no regrets," he said. "I did it the way it was supposed to be done, and I did it every single day. That's what I'm proudest of."

And he thought the ending, for a boy who was born in Canton, the birthplace of pro football, was perfect.

"For me, as a Northeast Ohio kid, to play his last game on the Cleveland Browns field in front of Cleveland Browns fans in a Cleveland Browns helmet," he said, "I couldn't write it any better."

Chris Spielman walked
away from the game with
his health and many
options for the future.

Just Plain Orange

BY DAN COUGHLIN

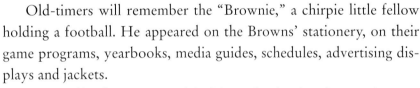

The Browns actually had a logo, a mascot of sorts, but Art Modell fired him.

Old-timers will remember the "Brownie," a chirpie little fellow holding a football. He appeared on the Browns' stationery, on their game programs, yearbooks, media guides, schedules, advertising displays and jackets.

In one of his first command decisions after buying the team in 1961, Model said, "Get rid of the little fellow." Or something like that.

Most people were comfortable with the Brownie. But Modell's opinion was the only one that counted. Still, even though the Brownie was yanked out of the spotlight, it never completely disappeared and would occasionally make cameo appearances on various collectibles. The Brownie enjoyed a brief comeback during the time Cleveland didn't have pro football, appearing on one of the most popular jackets in town during the Browns' absence.

While other teams have snazzed up their uniforms, put logos on their helmets and added cheerleaders to the sidelines, the Browns have gone in the other direction. They became more conservative.

In 1946, for example, when Arthur (Mickey) McBride founded the Browns, he formed an all-female band to entertain during lulls in the

LEFT: Outside the locker rooms under the stands of Cleveland Browns Stadium.

games. In fact, a picture in the old *Cleveland Press* in 1946 shows McBride leading the band like a drum major.

The early Browns also had cheerleaders, but they were short-lived. The girls' band also was disbanded and replaced by a men's band that survived until about 1970.

In the late 1970s the Browns introduced orange pants, but they were quietly discarded after a few years.

NFL Properties has periodically urged the Browns to adopt a helmet logo because it would increase the sale of licensed merchandise, but the organization steadfastly refused, claiming that the Browns are unique because they are the only team without a logo. One of the many traditions the new Browns ownership has respected is the franchise's distinction as the only one in the NFL to declare its helmets a logo-free zone.

Fred Gehrke of the Los Angeles Rams pioneered the helmet fashion statement in the late 1940s. A running back and wide receiver who worked as a commercial artist in the off-season, Gehrke decorated his helmet with the ram's horns that have been the trademark of the Rams for half a century.

With the introduction of solid plastic helmets in the 1950s, other teams followed. The Washington Redskins added arrows. The Green Bay Packers, Chicago Bears, San Francisco 49ers and New York Giants put initials on their helmets. The St. Louis Cardinals decorated their headgear with red cardinals. The Detroit Lions chose a catamount. The Pittsburgh Steelers borrowed the logo of the steel industry. The Philadelphia Eagles sprouted wings. It went on, sometimes to ridiculous extremes. The Cincinnati Bengals painted their entire helmets with tiger stripes.

The Browns stood firm. The Brownie was gone. What would be appropriate, a picture of Paul Brown's face on their helmets? Certainly not while Art Modell owned the team.

The white uniform with simple stripes and the unmarked orange helmet is fine for a franchise intent on building a bridge from the glorious 1950s to a new millennium. Unlike your typical expansion team, the Browns have a past. There is equity in those memories. Maybe Ty Detmer will not pass like Otto Graham and Terry Kirby will not run like Jim Brown, but they sure in blazes can look like them.

The orange, seal brown and white will never go out of style in Cleveland, a town where people still wear brown shoes and white socks to wedding receptions.

Cleveland is so old-fashioned, it is quaint. Think about this. Cleveland has a town square. No other major city has a town square. Cincinnati and Indianapolis have squares, but we're talking major cities here. Villages and hamlets have town squares with band shells and gazebos.

But downtown Cleveland, home to 50 major international corporations, is built around a town square. There are four grassy quadrants with flowers, trees, benches, statues to war heroes and founding fathers and a fountain that used to work. The Cleveland Orchestra has

LEFT AND RIGHT: Orange was the color of the day as fans welcomed the Browns home for their first preseason game in Cleveland Browns Stadium on August 21, 1999.

performed there, in the nostalgic manner of small-town Fourth of July band concerts and ice-cream socials. All public transportation emanates from the town square. Chipmunks live there, amidst thousands of daily pedestrians, hundreds of buses, fleets of cabs and convoys of trucks and automobiles.

Conservative Cleveland has been called the biggest small town in America and people like that. If the simple orange helmet means that Cleveland is a little bit square, that is a little bit all right. It is a badge of honor. That simple orange helmet symbolizes 10 straight championship games between 1946 and 1955. No other helmet, regardless of its logomania festoonery, splashed, swirls, rainbow-typographic artistry can make that claim.

LEFT: The Cleveland Orchestra draws a crowd for an outdoor concert.

ABOVE: Brittney Shaffer of Akron was among many young fans who made the Browns training camp in Berea a family affair.

"It was great day for Cleveland football. To come out and get a win just capped it off."

TIM COUCH

4. THE CANTON CONNECTION

A night to remember

BY RICH EXNER

Paul Brown must have been mighty proud looking down on Canton. On August 9, 1999 — next to the Pro Football Hall of Fame, where he is enshrined, and a city away from Paul Brown Tiger Stadium in Massillon, where he once coached high school football — the pro team bearing his name made its return. Fawcett Stadium was filled. The weather was perfect. The result right.

It was Browns 20, Cowboys 17.

Phil Dawson's 20-yard field goal at 11:42 p.m. finished things off — fittingly for those who suffered for so long without football — in overtime. ➤

PAGE 142: The Browns are introduced at the Hall of Fame Game.

PAGE 143: Browns players on the sidelines react to a good defensive play.

Less than four hours earlier, Dawson put his foot to the opening kickoff of the Hall of Fame Game, ending a three-season absence of the Browns from the NFL.

NFL Commissioner Paul Tagliabue compared the occasion to what it would be like if the Dodgers returned to Brooklyn.

Al Michaels, on ABC's national telecast, attempted to put Cleveland's temporary loss of the team in perspective by asking viewers to imagine the Eiffel Tower being moved from Paris to somewhere in Germany.

When it was over, Chris Palmer, the humble coach who could pass for a friendly guy operating an ice cream truck in Parma, directed attention to the faithful.

"This is for the fans of Cleveland. They've suffered three years without a team," Palmer said.

There was plenty of Browns orange to be seen throughout the stadium, from the fans to the helmets to the temporary plastic barricade

fencing, though skeptical Cowboys fans might say the fence color was a mere coincidence.

Thirty-seven-year-old Dave Bloomfield of Lorain told a tale that could be heard over and over. His game day getup, featuring orange pants, a No. 20 Browns jersey and a hard hat painted in the style of a Browns helmet, was recovered from storage before the game.

"I've had this stuff for 10 years. I put it all away when they announced they were leaving. ... I stopped watching football," said Bloomfield, a sea-

At 9 p.m. sharp, with 12:21 remaining in the second quarter, Couch brought the fans to their feet by merely stepping onto the field.

son ticket holder who took with him from the old stadium his bleacher plank. Section 62. Row 3. Seat 16.

Details of what happened on the field will fade quickly. After all, it was just an exhibition. The bigger picture of the return was what was important.

But for the record, some players permanently placed their names in the new history of the old team.

James Williams, playing on the kickoff team, made the first tackle. John Thierry made the first fumble recovery, which set up the first touchdown, a 1-yard leap by Terry Kirby.

The first flag fell when the Cowboys' Duane Hawthorne interfered with receiver Kevin Johnson at the 2, setting up Kirby's TD two plays later. And the first Browns' interception came when Corey Fuller picked off a Troy Aikman pass in the end zone later in the first quarter.

But the biggest first of all belonged to Tim Couch's debut.

At 9 p.m. sharp, with 12:21 remaining in the second quarter, Couch brought the fans to their feet by merely stepping onto the field. Then he made them gasp on his first play, barely overthrowing Johnson on a deep pass over the last Dallas defenders.

He later threw a 24-yard TD pass to Johnson and finished 11 of 17 for 137 yards and no interceptions.

John "Big Dawg" Thompson, frequently the face of Browns fans during the team's absence, spoke the thoughts of many from his front-row end-zone seat.

"I think the guy looks like a second-year player who is in mid-season form," Thompson said of the rookie Couch, who left Kentucky after his junior year.

Couch was just glad to help the festive atmosphere.

"It was great day for Cleveland football," Couch said afterward. "To come out and get a win just capped it off."

Paul Brown died in August 1991. But the tradition he started with the Browns was reborn in August 1999.

PAGE 148 AND 149: A record Hall of Fame Game crowd of 25,156 jammed Fawcett Stadium.

The Wizard of Oz

BY RICH EXNER

Ozzie Newsome became more dependable than the 1 o'clock Sunday kickoff. He caught passes in 150 consecutive games, more than anyone up to that point in NFL history except Steve Largent. He once went 557 rushes and receptions without fumbling. He is one of only five Browns to play in parts of three decades.

He was, to Browns fans everywhere, the Wizard of Oz.

So it was fitting that on the extended weekend in which the Browns made their triumphant return to the field, Newsome was in Canton being inducted into the Pro Football Hall of Fame. Who couldn't smile listening to the fans chant "Ozzz-ee, Ozzz-ee, Ozzz-ee" during the enshrinement ceremonies and again the night of the game, stoking memories of his fantastic catches in the retired stadium on the lakefront?

Sure, it was a mere coincidence, but fitting nonetheless. The statistically best and arguably greatest receiver in the history of the Browns had to wait through the team's absence before he could be inducted into the Hall of Fame.

He retired in 1990 and came up short of the votes needed for induction in his first three years of eligibility, 1996, 1997 and 1998, which directly coincided with the Browns' hiatus. But he was glad to be there in 1999. Ozzie repeatedly said how special it was to be part of the

Ozzie Newsome, who wore number 82, became the 14th member of the Browns to be enshrined in the Pro Football Hall of Fame.

The top three receiving seasons in Browns history belong to Newsome, with 89 catches in both 1983 and 1984, and 69 in 1981.

weekend in which "those orange helmets" would be back on the field.

Newsome certainly is a big part of that Browns tradition, catching more passes (662) than the next two players combined on the team's all-time list — Gary Collins (331) and Greg Pruitt (323).

The top three receiving seasons in Browns history belong to Newsome, with 89 catches in both 1983 and 1984, and 69 in 1981.

And he was the tight end for the Browns all three times (1986, 1987 and 1989) the team advanced to the AFC Championship Game.

Perhaps most impressive of all, he put together his huge numbers at a position not known for superstars before his arrival in the league. It wasn't until the 1988 induction of Mike Ditka that a tight end was enshrined in Canton.

Newsome left the game as the top receiving tight end in NFL history, a man recognized for changing the position with his ability to block well enough to play the line while possessing wide-receiver speed.

"You can be a good wide receiver in this league for a few years," Sam Rutigliano is quoted as telling his rookie end from Alabama in 1978. "But if you move to tight end, you can be a great tight end for a long time."

Twenty-one years later, Newsome became the 14th Browns player inducted into the Hall of Fame, joining Paul Warfield and Leroy Kelly as the only Browns honorees with no playing ties to Paul Brown.

The cradle of football

BY DAN COUGHLIN

Marion Motley was born on June 5, 1920, in Leesburg, Georgia, the county seat of rural Lee County.

Later that year, September 17, 1920, the National Football League was born in the back room of a Studebaker dealership in Canton, Ohio, the county seat of Stark County. The location was logical because three of the original 10 teams were from that area — the Cleveland Indians, the Akron Pros and the Canton Bulldogs, a nickname borrowed from Canton McKinley High School.

By the 1930s the National Football League was still struggling and so was the Motley family. The Depression spared no one, but it hit Leesburg harder than it hit Canton, which still had people working in factories and steel mills.

The Motley family moved to Canton and young Marion enrolled in the Canton schools. By the time Motley reached high school, small-town pro football was only a memory. Canton's last season in the NFL was 1926. Akron was gone. Even Cleveland was a revolving-door franchise, in and out of the league five times before Motley scored his first touchdown for the Canton McKinley Bulldogs in 1937. The following year Motley scored the first touchdown in the new 21,000-seat Fawcett Stadium, which was the largest high school football stadium in the country when it was dedicated.

Marion Motley was a powerful runner who also played linebacker early in his career.

Eight miles to the west in Massillon, Paul Brown was coaching Canton McKinley's arch rival, the Massillon Tigers, who dominated high school football with professional precision.

Brown was born in 1908 in Norwalk, a trucking town 50 miles west of Cleveland, but his family soon moved to Massillon, where he went through the public school system and, despite weighing only 130 pounds, went on to star on the gridiron at Washington High School, the official name of the school that is universally referred to as "Massillon."

Brown's success as the young head coach of his alma mater did not come overnight. Although he compiled a record of 80-8-2 in nine seasons, from 1932-40, he was almost fired after his first season, when he lost four games. Brown coached his first game at Massillon only a few days after celebrating his 24th birthday. Those who believed he was too young did not understand his long-range vision. Before long he owned the town. Over his last six seasons there he lost only one game. His Massillon teams won six mythical state championships and four mythical national championships.

He and Motley crossed paths twice, in 1937 and 1938, and Brown's Tigers beat Motley's Bulldogs both times in classic toe-to-toe Stark County Battles, 19-6 and 12-0. Although Brown prevailed over the massive fullback who could run like the wind, Brown never forgot him.

They would later collaborate in Cleveland to forge a bond between the Browns and the cities of Canton and Massillon.

In 1941 Brown went directly from Massillon to become head coach at Ohio State, where he compiled an 18-8-1 record and won a national championship in his second year, and then entered the Navy for the duration of World War II. Brown was commissioned a naval officer and assigned to coach the football team at Great Lakes Naval Training Station in Chicago, where his schedule included other military bases and

LEFT: Marion Motley.

ABOVE: The original Browns brain trust, led by Paul Brown, six months before the team's first game in 1946. From the left are John Brickels and Red Conkright, assistant coaches; Brown, the coach and general manager; Frosty Frobert, business manager; and assistants Fritz Heis and Bob Voigts.

Lou Groza (right), the
Browns' all-time leading
scorer, was enshrined in
the Pro Football Hall of
Fame in 1974, with his wife,
Jackie, and Berea Mayor
Stanley Trupo during
ceremonies dedicating Lou
Groza Boulevard in August
1999. The Browns'
headquarters is at 76 Lou
Groza Boulevard, the
number he wore during
many of his 21 seasons
with the Browns.

top college teams, including Ohio State and Notre Dame.

It was at Great Lakes that Brown and Motley were reunited, this time on the same side. Motley was the fullback on Brown's Navy team that crushed fifth-ranked Notre Dame 39-7 in the last game of the 1945 season.

Brown never returned to Ohio State, of course. In 1945, while still on duty with the Navy, he accepted an offer to become head coach of the Cleveland Browns at $25,000 a year, more than double what he had been making at Ohio State. Arthur B. Mickey McBride, the Browns' founding owner, sweetened the deal even further. Brown, who was making $100 a month as a lieutenant, was paid $1,000 a month until he was discharged and could go to work full time.

Brown wasted no time earning his money. While still in military uniform, he began contacting players he knew directly or by reputation. Instinctively, he returned to his coaching roots. The original Browns roster in 1946 consisted of 33 men and there were very few strangers. More than half had played for Brown or against him when he coached at Great Lakes, Ohio State and Massillon. No fewer than seven were former Buckeyes whom Brown had either coached or recruited, including Hall of Famers Lou Groza, Dante Lavelli and Bill Willis.

Also on his list was Motley, whose supporters could legitimately insist was the greatest all-around football player who ever lived. A powerful man of 232 pounds on a 6-foot 1-inch frame, Motley could match world-class sprinters stride for stride. He also was the finest blocker of

Members of the Groza family unveil the new marker for Lou Groza Boulevard.

his era, neutralizing defensive linemen like the Maginot Line. In his early years with the Browns, Motley also played linebacker on defense.

Like many players of that era whose professional careers were interrupted or postponed by World War II, Motley was a 26-year-old rookie in the Browns' inaugural season of 1946, but he went on to set the All-America Football Conference career rushing record during its four-year existence. When the Browns moved into the National Football League in 1950, Motley was once again the league rushing leader. He was inducted into the Pro Football Hall of Fame in 1968. Motley died June 27, 1999.

Chris Spielman received a hero's welcome when he was introduced before the first preseason game in Cleveland Browns Stadium.

Years later, two other Canton McKinley Bulldogs played for the Browns. They were defensive end Nick Roman (1972-74) and safety Ray Ellis (1986-87).

Needless to say, the Browns' original roster included familiar Massillon names as well. Lin Houston, who played on Brown's state championship team at Massillon and his national championship team at Ohio State, was the Browns' first starting right guard and earned a third ring in 1950 when the Browns won the NFL championship. He spent seven years with the Browns, from 1946-53. Houston's younger brother, Jim, later matched the trifecta with a state championship at Massillon, a national championship at Ohio State and the NFL championship with the Browns in 1964. Jim Houston was a Browns' linebacker from 1960-72.

In 1947 Brown added Horace Gillom, another former Massillon player, to his Cleveland roster. Gillom, a backup wide receiver, is best remembered as one of the game's all-time leading punters. For his career from 1947-55 Gillom averaged almost 44 yards a punt and led the NFL twice.

In 1948 Tommy James from Massillon began an eight-year career as a Browns defensive back and for several years was the holder for Lou Groza's extra points and field goals.

The Browns' historical link with Massillon almost was connected again in the summer of 1999 when linebacker Chris Spielman came out of retirement, but his last hurrah ended prematurely when a chronic spinal-cord condition forced him to turn in his cherished brown-and-orange uniform.

The Cleveland-Massillon Road remains open, however, for some future Brown to make the 50-mile journey from Paul Brown-Tiger Stadium to the new Cleveland Browns Stadium.

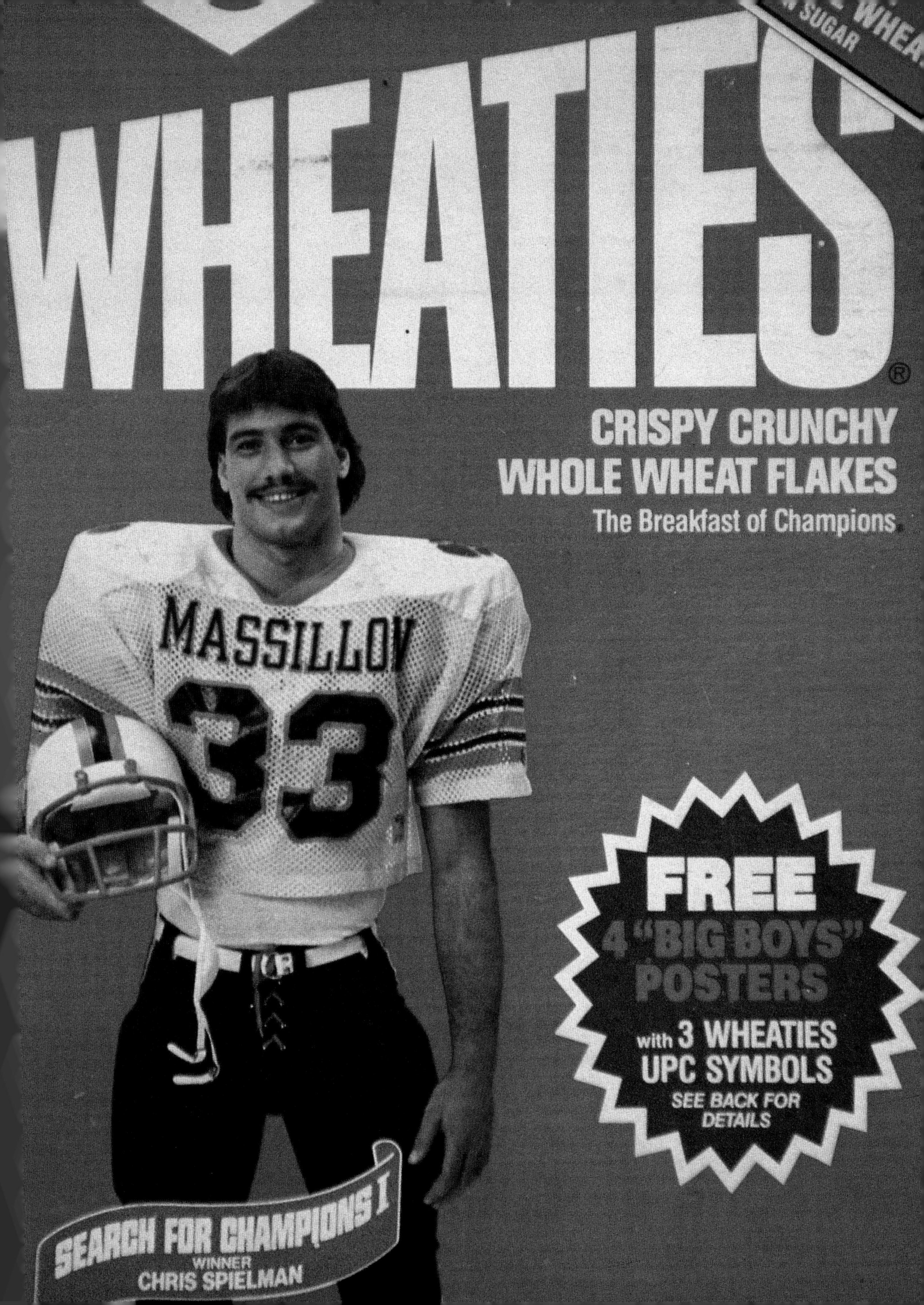
WHEATIES®
CRISPY CRUNCHY
WHOLE WHEAT FLAKES
The Breakfast of Champions.
MASSILLON
33
FREE
4 "BIG BOYS"
POSTERS
with 3 WHEATIES
UPC SYMBOLS
SEE BACK FOR
DETAILS
SEARCH FOR CHAMPIONS I
WINNER
CHRIS SPIELMAN

Browns in the Hall of Fame

Otto Graham, Enshrined 1965
The first Cleveland Browns player. Quarterback for seven of the Browns' eight championship teams. All-league nine of 10 years. Four touchdown passes in 1950 NFL title win. Ran for three touchdowns and passed for three more to win 1954 championship. Born Dec. 6, 1921 in Waukegan, Ill.

Paul Brown, Enshrined 1967
Organized the Browns in 1946. Built great Clevelant dynasty with 167-53-8 record, four AAFC titles, three NFL crowns, only one losing season in 17 years. Innovator with many coaching firsts to his credit. Born Sept. 7, 1908 in Norwalk, Ohio. Died Aug. 5, 1991.

Marion Motley, Enshrined 1968
Deadly pass blocker and feared runner during Browns' first eight seasons, 1946-1953. Also played linebacker early in career. All-time AAFC rushing champ. Top NFL rusher, 1950. Gained 4,720 yards, averaging 5.7 yards per carry, an all-time best. Born June 5, 1920 in Leesburg, Ga. Died June 27, 1999.

Jim Brown, Enshrined 1971
Syracuse All-America, 1965. Browns' No. 1 draft pick, 1957. Greatest runner in NFL history. Led NFL rushers eight years. All-NFL eight of nine years. NFL's MVP, 1958, 1965. Rookie of the year, 1957. Played in nine straight Pro Bowls. 12,312 yards rushing, 262 receptions, 15,459 combined net yards, 756 points scored. Born Feb. 17, 1936 in St. Simons, Ga.

Lou Groza, Enshrined 1974
Was last of the original Browns to retire after 1967 season. Played 21 years, missing 1960 because of a back injury. Played offensive tackle in addition to kicking most of his career. All-NFL tackle six years and NFL Player of the Year in 1954. Last-second field goal won 1950 title game. Browns' all-time leading scorer with1,608 points. Born Jan. 25, 1924 in Martins Ferry, Ohio.

Dante Lavelli, Enshrined 1975
Nicknamed "Glue Fingers," was top receiver in Browns' first 11 seasons, 1946-1956. Scored winning touchdown in 1946 championship game and caught 11 passes in 1950 title game. Caught 386 passes for 6,488 yards and 62 touchdowns. Had record 24 catches in six NFL title games.

Len Ford, Enshrined 1976
Great pass rusher and defensive end who was all-NFL five of eight seasons with the Browns, 1950-1957. Began as a two-way player in 1948 with the Los Angeles Dons of the AAFC, and retired after the 1958 season with Green Bay. Born Feb. 18, 1926 in Washington, D.C. Died March 14, 1972.

Bill Willis, Enshrined 1977
All-America tackle at Ohio State. Played both offense and defense during his eight-year career with the Browns, but excelled as defensive middle guard. Touchdown-saving tackle against New York Giants in 1950 was a key play in Browns' drive to their first NFL title. Born Oct. 5, 1921 in Columbus.

Bobby Mitchell, Enshrined 1983
Graceful halfback began career with the Browns, 1958-1961, and ended with the Washington Redskins, 1962-1968. Blessed with exceptional speed, balance and faking ability, he amassed 14,078 total yards and scored 91 touchdowns, eight of them kickoff returns. Born June 6, 1935, in Hot Springs, Ark.

Paul Warfield, Enshrined 1983
Wide receiver for the Browns, 1964-1969 and 1976-1977, and Miami Dolphins, 1970-1974. Dominant offensive player whose mere presence forced defensive adjustments. Caught 427 passes for 8,565 yards, a sensational 20.1 yards per catch, and scored 85 touchdowns. All-NFL five years and named to eight Pro Bowls. Born Nov. 28, 1942 in Warren, Ohio.

Mike McCormack, Enshrined 1984
Known for exceptional blocking skills during eight seasons an offensive tackle, 1955-1962, he played defense in 1954 and stole the ball to set up a key Browns touchdown in that year's championship game. Originally drafted by the New York Yanks in 1951 and played in the first of six Pro Bowls as a rookie. Missed the 1952-1953 seasons to service in the Army. Born June 21, 1930 in Chicago.

Frank Gatshi, Enshrined 1985
Great center who anchored powerful offensive line during the Browns' first 11 seasons, and retired after a championship season with the Lions in 1957. Never missed a game or practice in high school, college or the pros. Played in 11 championship games in 11 years, winning eight times. Born March 18, 1922 in Farmington, W.Va.

Leroy Kelly, Enshrined 1994
Eight-round draft pick out of Morgan State in 1964, became dominant NFL runner after Jim Brown's retirement. 1,000-yard rusher three times, 1966-1968. Retired after 1973 season with 7,274 yards rushing, 2,281 receiving and 2,774 returning, for 12,329 total yares and 90 touchdowns. Born May 20, 1942 in Philadelphia.

Ozzie Newsome, Enshrined 1999
Browns' first-round draft pick out of Alabama, 1978. Nicknamed "Wizard of Oz," Retired after 13 seasons as all-time leading tight end receiver. Caught pass in 150 consecutive games. Scored 47 touchdowns on 662 receptions for 7,980 yards. Born March 16, 1956, in Muscle Shoals, Ala.

LEFT: Otto Graham, who became the first NFL player to wear a face mask, played most of his career without one. That changed after Graham was injured in a violent confrontation with two 49er defenders during the first half a game in 1953. It took 15 stiches to close the gash on Graham's face, but he returned in the third quarter to lead his team to victory after Paul Brown rigged Graham's helmet with a clear plastic bar in front of his face. The device soon evolved into the face mask.

"I'll go in, but I've got to have the best coach and the best players in the country. I've got to have the best promotion, too."

—ARTHUR MCBRIDE, ON HIS DECISION TO BE THE
FIRST OWNER OF THE CLEVELAND BROWNS

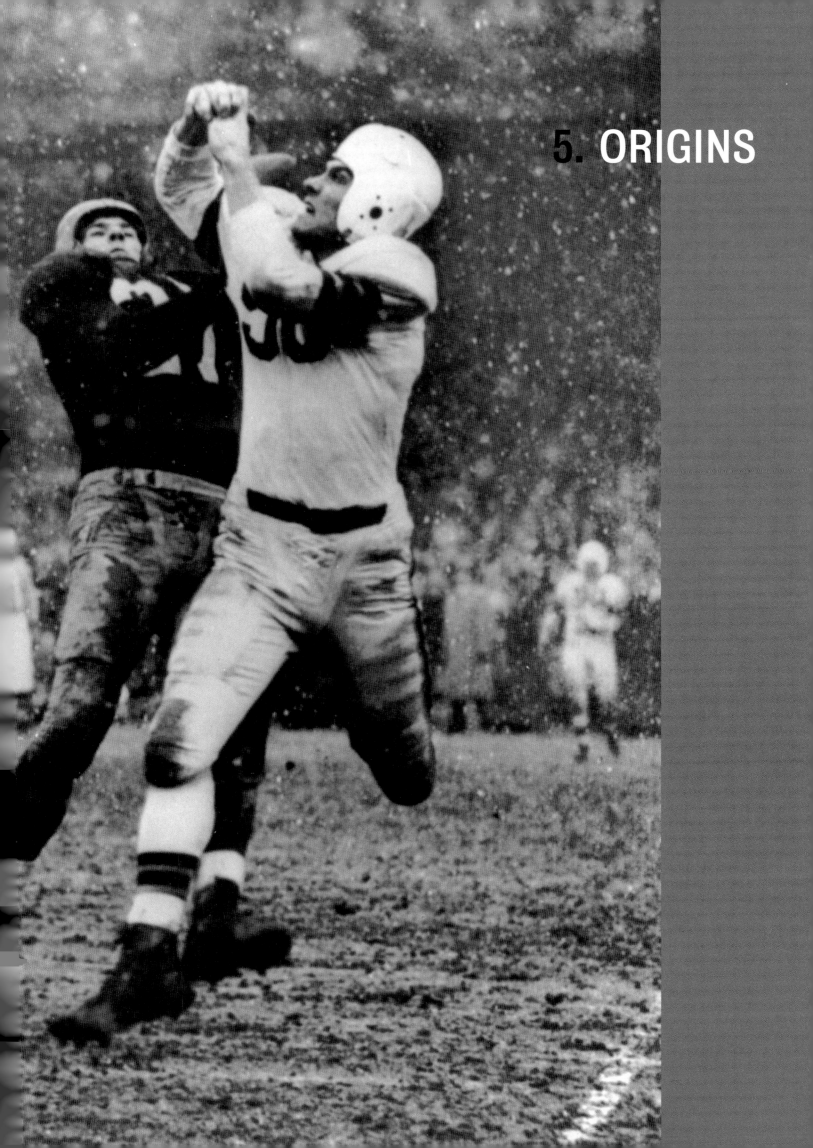

5. ORIGINS

Fireworks marked the birth of
original Browns
BY TIM GRAHAM

PAGE 166: The Browns' first owner, Arthur "Mickey" McBride, was a showman who gave fans more than championship football.

PAGE 167: Dante Lavelli, known as "Glue Fingers" during his Hall of Fame career, scored the winning touchdown in the 1946 AAFC title game. He now owns a furniture store in Rocky River.

The Cleveland Browns were born in 1946, after the 1945 NFL champion Cleveland Rams moved to Los Angeles. The Rams in 1945 drew just 72,000 spectators to four regular-season home games.

"The reason I'm moving to Los Angeles is that I believe it will become the greatest professional football town in America," Rams owner Dan Reeves told the Associated Press at the time. Another reason was that Cleveland newspapers were already giving prominent coverage to the development of Cleveland's entry into the new All-America Football Conference. ➤

Team owner Arthur B. "Mickey" McBride made headlines by hiring Paul Brown to coach the team. Brown was already on his way to becoming a legend. He was just 24 when he became coach of the Massillon High School team and 33 when he began coaching the Ohio State Buckeyes, a team he had led to the national championship.

Brown began making headlines by assembling an array of talent anchored by players who had played for or against him at Massillon, Ohio State and, during World War II, the Great Lakes Naval Training Center.

The franchise's first nickname, picked in a contest sponsored by a Cleveland newspaper, was the Panthers. Published accounts offer two reasons for the change to the Browns before the team began play in the new league.

Both involve the fact that a semipro team called the Panthers had failed in Cleveland some years earlier. Upon learning about the old Panthers, Paul Brown supposedly insisted on a change, saying he did not want his team associated in any way with failure. Another reason is that someone claiming to own the rights to the Panthers' name wanted McBride to buy it, and he balked at the idea. In any case, naming the team the Browns, in honor of their already-famous coach, had been a popular suggestion in the naming contest. And so they became the Browns.

By the time they made their debut, on September 6, 1946, McBride had invested $260,000 in the team. It pales against the $530 million franchise fee for the new Browns, but it was a staggering sum at the time. The opening-night game was eagerly anticipated and heavily promoted. In addition to football talent, McBride promised fireworks and the spectacular Musical Majorettes, a group of 30 to 35 young women who were featured prominently in the Browns' promotional efforts.

The opening game drew a crowd of 60,145 to Municipal Stadium. It's believed to have been the largest crowd ever to attend a professional football game up to that point, and was almost double the 32,178

The Browns' 1946 debut was national news. This photograph of the opening kickoff appeared in *Life* magazine September 23, 1946.

RIGHT: McBride and Paul Brown in 1948 after the Browns won their third consecutive AAFC title.

who witnessed the 1945 NFL title game in Cleveland. Otto Graham did not start the game, saying the honor should go to hometown hero Cliff Lewis from Lakewood. Three and a half minutes into the game, Lewis tossed a 16-yard pass to Mac Speedie for the Browns' first score in a 44-0 rout of the Miami Seahawks.

Tickets that first year were priced at $3.60 and $2.40 per game. Season-ticket packages cost $21.60 or $14.40, offering seven games for the price of six.

1999 **season firsts**

First kickoff in Cleveland Browns Stadium
Chris Gardocki, Browns, 70 yards for a
    touchback, September 12

First play from scrimmage in Cleveland Browns Stadium
Kordell Stewart, Steelers, incomplete pass,
    September 12

First run in Cleveland Browns Stadium
Jerome Bettis, Steelers, 6 yards, September 12

First tackle in Cleveland Browns Stadium
Marquez Pope, Browns, September 12

First pass completion in Cleveland Browns Stadium
Kordell Stewart to Richard Huntley, Steelers,
    7 yards, September 12

First Browns offensive play
Ty Detmer pass to Leslie Shepherd, 13 yards,
    September 12

First Browns run
Marc Edwards, 1 yard, September 12

First interception in Cleveland Browns Stadium
Chris Oldham, Steelers, pass from Ty
    Detmer, September 12

First touchdown in Cleveland Browns Stadium
Kordell Stewart, Pittsburgh, 1 yard run,
    September 12

First extra point in Cleveland Browns Stadium
Kris Brown, Pittsburgh, September 12

First punt in Cleveland Browns Stadium
Chris Gardocki, Browns, 45 yards, September 12

First penalty in Cleveland Browns Stadium
John Thierry, Browns, face mask, 5 yards,
    September 12

First field goal in Cleveland Browns Stadium
Kris Brown, Steelers, 18 yards, September 12

First quarterback sack in Cleveland Browns Stadium
Jason Gildon, Steelers, tackles Ty Detmer for
    6-yard loss, September 12

First sack by the Browns
Derrick Alexander tackles Kordell Stewart
    for 12-yard loss, September 12

First ejection from the Dawg Pound
Six uniformed police officers remove one
    unruly fan, 8:46 p.m., September 12

First Browns score
Phil Dawson, field goal, 41 yards with 6:50
    left in First half, at Tennessee, September
    19

First Browns touchdown
Kevin Johnson, 39 yards, pass from Tim
    Couch, 2:51 left in third quarter at
    Tennessee, September 19

First Browns touchdown in Cleveland Browns Stadium
Kevin Johnson, 64 yards, pass from Tim
    Couch, 8:53 left in First quarter vs. New
    England, October 3

First Browns third-down conversion
Tim Couch, 15-yard run, on a third and 3, at
    Tennessee, September 19

First interception by the Browns
Daylon McCutcheon off Stoney Case, at
    Baltimore, September 26

First fumble recovery by the Browns
McNeil off Terry Glenn fumble, 8:53 left in
    First quarter vs. New England, October 3

First Browns victory
21-16 at New Orleans, October 31, 1999,
    after 56-yard Hail Mary TD pass from Tim
    Couch to Kevin Johnson as time expired.

Kevin Johnson races
toward the end zone for
the Browns' first
regular-season
touchdown in Cleveland
Browns Stadium against
New England, October 3,
1999.

History of the Cleveland Browns

1946: Browns were started by owner Arthur (Mickey) McBride as member of the All-America Football Conference. Paul Brown was named coach and general manager and the first player he signed was then tailback Otto Graham. The Browns won the Western title with a 42-17 victory over the Buffalo Bisons and then defeated the New York Yankees in the championship game (14-9).

1947-49: Browns continued their domination of the AAFC, winning three more championships.

1950: Following the merger of the AAFC and the NFL, the Browns tied with the New York Giants with 10-2 records for a share of Eastern title. Browns won playoff, 8-3, and then stopped Los Angeles, 30-28, for the championship.

1951-53: Browns won three consecutive Eastern titles, but lost each time in the league's title match, once to Los Angeles and twice to Detroit. In 1953, McBride sold the club to an organization headed by David Jones.

1954-55: Led by quarterback Otto Graham, the Browns won back-to-back NFL championships, defeating Detroit and Los Angeles.

1956: At 5-7, the Browns suffered first losing season.

1957: Jim Brown was drafted; was named rookie of the year and helped Cleveland to Eastern Division title.

1961: Art Modell purchased the Browns for the then unheard of sum of $4 million.

1963: Blanton Collier, a Browns' assistant, was named head coach.

1964: Browns win division title with 52-20 victory over Giants and captured NFL championship with 27-0 win over Colts.

1965: In his last season, Jim Brown won NFL MVP honors and led Cleveland to NFL title game where they were defeated by Green Bay.

1966: An eighth round pick from 1964, Leroy Kelly became the club's dominant threat, rushing for 1,141 yards, but the Browns finished second in their division to Dallas.

1968: With newly acquired quarterback Bill Nelsen (from Pittsburgh), Browns won division; beat Dallas in playoffs and lost to Baltimore in the championship.

1969: Browns won third consecutive division crown, but lost to Minnesota in title game.

1970: Browns became members of AFC Central Division and finished second. The Browns beat the New York Jets on Monday Night Football's first-ever telecast.

1971: Nick Skorich, a Browns' assistant, was named head coach. Team won first AFC Central crown.

1972: Browns once again gained postseason, losing to eventual champion Miami in playoffs, 20-14, as Dolphins complete undefeated season.

1975-77: Forrest Gregg, Browns' offensive line coach, becomes head coach; Greg Pruitt has three consecutive 1,000-yard rushing seasons; Dick Modzelewski coaches final game of 1977.

1978: Sam Rutigliano becomes the first non-Browns' assistant to gain head coaching position. Team won first three on way to 8-8 finish.

Gary Collins (86), perhaps the greatest Browns receiver not in the Hall of Fame, could not hold on to this pass, which would have gone for a touchdown in a 1964 game against Detroit. Photographer Ron Kuntz captured this sequence showing Collins surrounded by Lions defenders Bobby Thompson (27) and Yale Lary (28).

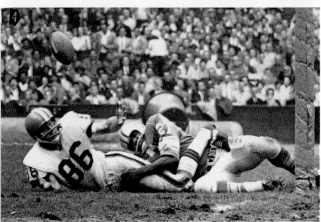

1979: Losses in final two games prevented team from entering playoffs, finishing 9-7; Mike Pruitt keeps the tradition of outstanding Browns' running backs and has the first of three straight 1,000-yard seasons.

1980: Browns win AFC Central title with 11-5 record; lost to eventual Super Bowl champion Oakland in playoff; Brian Sipe is consensus MVP of league.

1982: In strike-shortened season, Browns finish eighth in AFC (4-5) and gain playoffs second time in three years. Lost to Raiders in Super Bowl Tournament.

1983: Browns tied for wildcard playoff spot with 9-7 record, but lost NFL tie-breaking procedure to Denver and Seattle.

1984: Browns replaced head coach Sam Rutigliano with defensive coordinator Marty Schottenheimer after a 1-7 midseason record and finished season at 5-11. TE Ozzie Newsome caught 89 passes for second straight year.

1985: Browns captured their third Central Division championship, but lost to Dolphins, 24-21, in Miami. Rookie Kevin Mack (1,104) and Earnest Byner (1,002) each gained 1,000 yards rushing. It marked the third time in 66-year history of NFL that teammates both rushed for over 1,000 yards in the same season.

1986: Browns won more games than ever before during regular season, finishing 12-4 en route to their second consecutive AFC Central crown. In a double-overtime playoff thriller before a packed Cleveland Stadium crowd, the Browns beat the New York Jets, 23-20, to advance to the AFC championship game. The Browns lose to Denver, also in overtime, 23-20.

1987: Browns capture their third straight AFC Central crown, as they finished the season 10-5. The third week of the NFL season was cancelled due to the 24-day players' strike, while three "replacement" games were played (the Browns went 2-1). The Browns defeated the Colts, 38-21, at Cleveland Stadium in the AFC playoffs, then dropped their second straight AFC Championship to Denver despite a spectacular come-from-behind bid that saw them score 30 second-half points, only to fall, 38-33 in Mile High Stadium. Bernie Kosar wins the AFC passing title with a 95.4 QB rating, and an NFL-high eight Browns make the Pro Bowl.

1988: Cleveland finishes 10-6 and earns a Wild Card berth by defeating Houston, 28-23, in the season finale by overcoming a 16-point third-quarter deficit. Houston defeats the Browns, 24-23, in the Wild Card game played on Christmas Eve. Four Cleveland quarterbacks suffered injuries during the course of the season. Marty Schottenheimer resigns on Dec. 27.

1989: Owner Art Modell announces Bud Carson as the Browns' seventh full-time head coach on January 27. The Browns

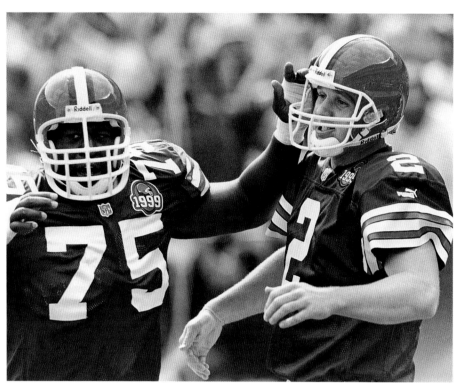

Offensive lineman Lomas Brown and quarterback Tim Couch celebrate the Browns' first 1999 regular-season touchdown in Cleveland Browns Stadium, October 3, 1999.

win their fourth division title in five years with a 9-6-1 record, and advance to the playoffs for an AFC-high fifth straight season. Browns advance to third title game in four years by defeating Buffalo, 34-30, but lose to Denver, 37-21, at Mile High Stadium in AFC Championship.

1990: Browns suffer worst season in franchise history, finishing 3-13. Jim Shofner replaces Bud Carson as interim head coach on November 5.

1991-93: Owner Art Modell announces Bill Belichick as the eighth full-time head coach on February 5, 1991. Browns move into new training and administrative complex, located in Berea, Ohio, in August, 1991 and hold training camp there in July, 1992. Browns finish 6-10, 7-9 and 7-9, respectively. Unrestricted free agency begins in 1993. Browns sign five players in first year of system, including quarterback Vinny Testaverde of Tampa Bay.

1994: The Browns earn a playoff berth for the first time in the '90s, finishing 11-5 and defeating the New England Patriots, 20-13, in the Wild Card game at soldout Cleveland Stadium. The Browns faced the Steelers for the first time ever in the playoffs, and lost 29-9 at Three Rivers Stadium. The Cleveland defense sets a team record by allowing just 204 points, and six players go to the Pro Bowl. Leroy Kelly becomes 13th Brown to enter Hall of Fame on July 30.

1995: The Browns concluded the season with a 5-11 record. In November, owner Art Modell announced he was relocating his franchise to Baltimore, Md. The final

game played at Cleveland Municipal Stadium was on Sunday, December 17, 1995 against the Cincinnati Bengals. The Browns defeated the Bengals, 26-10. The victory marked an all-time NFL season record of 202-117-5 (.631) while playing at Cleveland Municipal Stadium.

1996: The City of Cleveland and the NFL secured an unprecedented deal to return the Cleveland Browns to the playing field in 1999. The deal stipulated that the name, colors and heritage of the Browns would remain in Cleveland.

1998: The NFL awards the Cleveland Browns to Alfred Lerner and Carmen Policy on September 8, 1999. The NFL formally transfers ownership of Cleveland Browns to Lerner and Policy on October 23, 1999. Dwight Clark is named Vice President, Director of Football Operations on November 30, 1999.

1999: Chris Palmer is named the ninth full-time head coach in Cleveland Browns history January 21, 1999. The Browns are awarded the rights to the first pick in the 1999 NFL Draft and use the pick to select Kentucky quarterback Tim Couch. The first pre-season game in Cleveland Browns Stadium is played on August 21, with the Browns losing to Minnesota, 28-21. The Browns open the regular season at home on September 12, losing to Pittsburgh, 43-0.

Bernie Kosar, one of the most popular players in the history of the Browns, braved all kinds of weather during his tenure with the team, 1985-1993. He continues to serve the Browns as a consultant.

Cleveland Browns records, 1950-1995*

LONGEST PLAYS

Long Runs From Scrimmage
90 — Bobby Mitchell vs. Washington, Nov. 15, 1959 (TD)
80 — Jim Brown vs. Washington, Sept. 15, 1963 (TD)
78 — Greg Pruitt vs. Kansas City, Oct. 30, 1977 (TD)
77 — Mike Pruitt vs. Oakland, Dec. 9, 1979 (TD)
73 — Ernie Green vs. Detroit, Dec. 8, 1963
71 — Jim Brown vs. Philadelphia, Nov. 23, 1960 (TD)
71 — Jim Brown vs. Dallas, Sept. 22, 1963 (TD)
71 — Jim Brown vs. Dallas, Oct. 18, 1964
71 — Mike Pruitt vs. Buffalo, Oct. 29, 1978 (TD)

Long Forward Passes
97 — Bernie Kosar to Webster Slaughter vs. Chi. Bears, Oct. 23, 1989 (TD)
87 — Bill Nelsen to Milt Morin vs. Philadelphia, Nov. 24, 1968
86 — Milt Plum to Leon Clarke vs. Philadelphia, Oct. 23, 1960 (TD)
83 — Frank Ryan to Jim Brown vs. Washington, Sept. 15, 1963 (TD)
82 — Bill Nelsen to Paul Warfield vs. St. Louis, Dec. 14, 1969 (TD)
81 — Otto Graham to Dub Jones vs. San Francisco, Sept. 30, 1951 (TD)
81 — Vinny Testaverde to Derrick Alexander vs. Arizona, Sept. 18, 1994 (TD)
80 — Otto Graham to Dub Jones vs. Pittsburgh, Oct. 29, 1950 (TD)
80 — Frank Ryan to Walter Roberts vs. Washington, Sept. 19, 1965 (TD)
80 — Mike Phipps to Frank Pitts vs. N.Y. Jets, Dec. 17, 1972 (TD)
80 — Bernie Kosar to Webster Slaughter vs. Houston, Oct. 29, 1989 (TD)

Long Punt Returns
92 — Eric Metcalf at Cincinnati, Sept. 4, 1994 (TD)
91 — Eric Metcalf vs. Pittsburgh, Oct. 24, 1993 (TD)
84 — Gerald McNeil vs. Detroit, Sept. 28, 1986 (TD)
78 — Bobby Mitchell vs. New York, Dec. 6, 1959 (TD)
75 — Eric Metcalf vs. Chicago Bears, Nov. 29, 1992 (TD)
75 — Eric Metcalf vs. Pittsburgh, Oct. 24, 1993 (TD)
74 — Leroy Kelly vs. Denver, Oct. 24, 1971
73 — Eric Metcalf vs. Cincinnati, Oct. 23, 1994 (TD)
72 — Greg Pruitt vs. Denver, Oct. 27, 1974
69 – Derrick Alexander vs. Buffalo Bills, Oct. 2, 1995
68 — Bobby Mitchell vs. Philadelphia, Nov. 23, 1958 (TD)
68 — Leroy Kelly vs. New York, Oct. 25, 1964 (TD)

Long Punts
80 — Horace Gillom vs. New York, Nov. 28, 1954
75 — Horace Gillom vs. Pittsburgh, Oct. 29, 1950
73 — Horace Gillom vs. Washington, Oct. 26, 1952
73 — Gary Collins vs. Pittsburgh, Oct. 5, 1963
73 — Brian Hansen vs. Denver, Sept. 27, 1992
72 — Brian Hansen at Cincinnati, Oct. 17, 1993
71 — Gary Collins vs. Philadelphia, Oct. 2, 1965
71 — Don Cockroft vs. Houston, Nov. 22, 1970
71 — Don Cockroft vs. Kansas City, Dec. 2, 1973
70 — Fred Morrison vs. Baltimore, Nov. 11 1956

Long Kickoff Return
104 — Carl Ward vs. Washington, Nov. 26, 1967 (TD)
102 — Leroy Bolden vs. Chi. Cardinals, Oct. 26, 1958 (TD)
101 — Eric Metcalf at Houston, Dec. 9, 1990 (TD)
100 — Gerald McNeil at Pittsburgh, Oct. 5, 1986 (TD)
98 — Bobby Mitchell vs. Philadelphia, Nov. 23, 1958 (TD)
98 — Eric Metcalf at New York Jets, Sept. 16, 1990 (TD)
94 — Homer Jones vs. New York Jets, Sept. 21, 1970 (TD)
92 — Billy Lefear vs. Cincinnati, Nov. 23, 1975
91 — Bobby Mitchell vs. Philadelphia Nov. 19, 1961 (TD)
90 — Bobby Mitchell vs. Dallas, Oct. 16, 1960 (TD)
90 — Eric Metcalf vs. Buffalo, Jan. 6, 1990 (TD) (Playoff)

Long Interception Returns
97 — Najee Mustafaa vs. Miami, Oct. 10, 1993 (TD)
93 — Eric Turner vs. Arizona, Sept. 18, 1994 (TD)
92 — Bernie Parrish vs. Chicago, Dec. 11, 1960 (TD)
92 — David Brandon vs. Chicago, Nov. 29, 1992 (TD)
88 — Ross Fichtner (lateral from Erich Barnes) vs. New Orleans, Oct. 1, 1967
88 — Walt Sumner vs. Dallas, Dec. 28, 1969 (TD) (Playoff)
79 — Jim Houston vs. New York, Dec. 3, 1967 (TD)
75 — Brian Washington at Pittsburgh, Oct. 2, 1988 (TD)
70 — Johnny Brewer vs. Washington, Nov. 26, 1967 (TD)
68 — Mike Howell vs. Washington, Dec. 19, 1971
68 — Felix Wright vs. L.A. Rams, Oct. 26, 1987

Long Field Goals
65 — Walter Beach vs. Detroit, Nov. 15, 1964 (TD)
65 — Chip Banks vs. New England, Nov. 20, 1983 (TD)
64 — Mike Johnson vs. San Diego, Sept. 23, 1990 (TD)

Long Fumble Returns
89 — Don Paul vs. Pittsburgh, Nov. 10, 1957 (TD)
73 — Stevon Moore at Houston, Nov. 8, 1992 (TD)
55 — Earnest Byner vs. Buffalo, Nov. 4, 1984 (TD)
54 — Len Ford vs. Philadelphia, Nov. 13, 1955
47 — George Young vs. Washington, Oct. 14, 1951 (TD)
47 — Nick Roman vs. Denver, Oct. 27, 1974
44 — Junior Wren vs. Chi. Cardinals, Oct. 4, 1959 (TD)
42 — Jerry Helluin vs. Philadelphia, Oct. 10, 1953 (TD)
39 — Chuck Noll vs. Green Bay, Nov. 4, 1956 (TD)
38 — Horace Gillom vs. Pittsburgh, Oct. 21, 1951 (TD)
37 — Tom James vs. Chi. Cardinals, Nov. 29, 1953 (TD)
37 — Vince Newsome at Washington, Oct. 13, 1991 (TD)

Long Field Goals
60 — Steve Cox vs. Cincinnati, Oct. 21, 1984
58 — Steve Cox vs. Denver, Dec. 4, 1983
57 — Don Cockroft vs. Denver, Oct. 29, 1972
55 — Matt Stover at Houston, Nov. 17, 1991
53 — Matt Stover at Houston, Dec. 12, 1993
52 — Matt Bahr at Minnesota, Oct. 26, 1986
52 — Matt Bahr vs. L.A. Raiders, Jan. 8, 1983 (Playoff)
52 — Lou Groza vs. Los Angeles, Dec. 23, 1951 (Playoff)
52 — Lou Groza vs. N.Y. Giants, Oct. 12, 1952
51 — Lou Groza vs. Chi. Cardinals, Dec. 16, 1956
51 — Lou Groza vs. Pittsburgh, Oct. 28, 1962
51 — Don Cockroft vs. St. Louis, Oct. 28, 1979
51 — Matt Stover vs. Pittsburgh, Oct. 11, 1992
50 — Lou Groza vs. Pittsburgh, Nov. 22, 1953
50 — Don Cockroft vs. St. Louis, Dec. 14, 1968
50 — Don Cockroft vs. Pittsburgh, Oct. 10, 1976
50 — Matt Bahr vs. Cincinnati, Oct. 21, 1984
50 — Matt Bahr at Miami, Oct. 8, 1989
50 — Matt Stover vs. Philadelphia, Nov. 10, 1991

* These records do not include the four seasons the Browns played in the All-America Football Conference, 1946-1949.

- 177 -

CLEVELAND BROWNS INDIVIDUAL RECORDS

SERVICE

Most Seasons
17 Lou Groza (1950-59, 61-67)
16 Clay Matthews (1978-93)
15 Gene Hickerson (1958-60, 62-73)

Most Consecutive Seasons
16 Clay Matthews (1978-93)
14 Doug Dieken (1971-84)
13 Don Cockroft (1968-80)
13 Jim Houston (1960-72)
13 Dick Schafrath (1959-71)
13 Clarence Scott (1971-83)
13 Ozzie Newsome (1978-90)
12 Gene Hickerson (1962-73)
12 Walter Johnson (1965-76)
12 Ray Renfro (1952-63)
12 Jerry Sherk (1970-81)

Most Games
232 Clay Matthews (1978-93)
216 Lou Groza (1950-59, 61-67)
203 Doug Dieken (1971-84)
202 Gene Hickerson (1958-60, 62-73)

Most Consecutive Games
203 Doug Dieken (1971-84)
188 Don Cockroft (1968-80)
178 Clarence Scott (1971-83)
168 Walter Johnson (1965-76)
165 Gene Hickerson (1962-73)

Most Consecutive Starts
194 Doug Dieken (1971-84)

SCORING

Most Points - Career
1,345 Lou Groza (1950-59,1961-67); 233 FG, 640 PAT, 1 TD
1,080 Don Cockroft (1968-80); 216 FG, 432 PAT
756 Jim Brown (1957-65); 126 TD
677 Matt Bahr (1981-89); 143 FG, 248 PAT
540 Leroy Kelly (1964-73); 90 TD

Most Points - Season
126 Jim Brown (1965); 21 TD
120 Leroy Kelly (1968); 20 TD
115 Lou Groza (1964); 22 FG, 49 PAT
110 Matt Stover (1994); 26 FG, 32 PAT
108 Jim Brown (1962); 18 TD
108 Jim Brown (1958); 18 TD
108 Lou Groza (1953); 23 FG, 39 PAT

Most Points - Game
36 Dub Jones (11/25/1951 vs. Chicago Bears); 6 TD
30 Jim Brown (11/01/1959 at Baltimore Colts); 5 TD
24 Eric Metcalf (09/20/1992 at Los Angeles Raiders); 4 TD
24 Leroy Kelly (12/01/1968 vs. New York Giants); 4 TD
24 Jim Brown (11/28/1965 at Pittsburgh Steelers); 4 TD
24 Jim Brown (11/18/1962 vs. St. Louis Cardinals); 4 TD
24 Jim Brown (11/19/1961 vs. Philadelphia Eagles); 4 TD
24 Jim Brown (10/26/1958 at Chicago Cardinals); 4 TD
24 Jim Brown (11/24/1957 vs. Los Angeles Rams); 4 TD

Most Consecutive Games Scoring
107 Lou Groza (1950) 9 – (1959) 2

Most Seasons, 100 or More Points
3 Jim Brown (1958, 62, 65)

Most Total TDs - Career
126 Jim Brown (1957-65); 106 Rush, 20 Recv
90 Leroy Kelly (1964-73); 74 Rush, 13 Recv, 3 Ret
70 Gary Collins (1962-71); 70 Recv
55 Ray Renfro (1952-63); 4 Rush, 50 Recv, 1 Ret
54 Kevin Mack (1985-93); 46 Rush, 8 Recv

Most Total TDs - Season
21 Jim Brown (1965); 17 Rush, 4 Recv
20 Leroy Kelly (1968); 16 Rush, 4 Recv
18 Jim Brown (1962); 13 Rush, 5 Recv
18 Jim Brown (1958); 17 Rush, 1 Recv
16 Leroy Kelly (1966); 15 Rush, 1 Recv

Most Total TDs - Game
6 Dub Jones (11/25/1951 vs. Chicago Bears); 4 Rush, 2 Recv
5 Jim Brown (11/01/1959 at Baltimore Colts); 5 Rush
4 Eric Metcalf (09/20/1992 at Los Angeles Raiders); 1 Rush, 3 Recv
4 Leroy Kelly (12/01/1968 vs. New York Giants); 4 Rush
4 Jim Brown (11/28/1965 at Pittsburgh Steelers); 3 Rush, 1 Recv
4 Jim Brown (11/18/1962 vs. St. Louis Cardinals); 4 Rush
4 Jim Brown (11/19/1961 vs. Philadelphia Eagles); 4 Rush
4 Jim Brown (10/26/1958 at Chicago Cardinals); 4 Rush
4 Jim Brown (11/24/1957 vs. Los Angeles Rams); 4 Rush

Most Consecutive Games Scoring Touchdowns
10 Jim Brown (1965)
9 Leroy Kelly (1968)

Most Return TDs - Career
7 Eric Metcalf (1989-94)
6 Bobby Mitchell (1958-61)
5 Warren Lahr (1950-59)
5 Ken Konz (1953-59)
4 Bernie Parrish (1959-66)

Most Return TDs - Season
2 Eric Metcalf (1994)
2 Eric Metcalf (1993)
2 David Brandon (1992)
2 Eric Metcalf (1990)
2 Thane Gash (1989)
2 David Grayson (1989)
2 Gerald McNeil (1986)
2 Jim Houston (1967)
2 Leroy Kelly (1965)
2 Bobby Mitchell (1961)
2 Bobby Franklin (1960)
2 Bobby Mitchell (1958)
2 Ken Konz (1954)
2 Warren Lahr (1951)
2 Warren Lahr (1950)

Most Return TDs - Game
2 Eric Metcalf (10/24/1993 vs. Pittsburgh Steelers)
2 David Grayson (09/10/1989 at Pittsburgh Steelers)
2 Bobby Franklin (12/11/1960 vs. Chicago Bears)
2 Bobby Mitchell (11/23/1958 vs. Philadelphia Eagles)

Most Extra Points - Career
640 Lou Groza (1950-59,1961-67)
432 Don Cockroft (1968-80)
248 Matt Bahr (1981-89)
149 Matt Stover (1991-95)
44 Sam Baker (1960-61)

Most Extra Points - Season
51 Lou Groza (1966)
49 Lou Groza (1964)
46 Don Cockroft (1968)
45 Don Cockroft (1969)
45 Lou Groza (1965)

Most Extra Points - Game
8 Lou Groza (12/06/1953 vs. New York Giants)
7 Lou Groza (12/04/1966 vs. New York Giants)
7 Lou Groza (12/12/1964 at New York Giants)
7 Lou Groza (10/19/1952 at Philadelphia Eagles)
7 Lou Groza (12/02/1951 vs. Chicago Cardinals)

Most Consecutive Extra Points Made
138 Lou Groza (1963-66)

Most Field Goals - Career
233 Lou Groza (1950-59,1961-67)
216 Don Cockroft (1968-80)
143 Matt Bahr (1981-89)
108 Matt Stover (1991-95)
14 Jerry Kauric (1990)

Most Field Goals - Season
29 Matt Stover (1995)
26 Matt Stover (1994)
24 Matt Bahr (1988)
24 Matt Bahr (1984)
23 Lou Groza (1953)

Most Field Goals - Game
5 Matt Stover (10/29/1995 at Cincinnati Bengals)
5 Don Cockroft (10/19/1975 at Denver Broncos)

Most Consecutive Games Field Goal Made
14 Lou Groza (1950) 10 (1951) 4

Most Consecutive Field Goals Made
23 Matt Stover (1994) 20 (1995) 3
16 Don Cockroft (1974) 11 (1975) 5

Highest Field Goal Pct - Career (minimum 50 attempts)
81.20 Matt Stover (1991-95); 133-108
74.09 Matt Bahr (1981-89); 193-143
65.85 Don Cockroft (1968-80); 328-216
58.10 Lou Groza (1950-59,1961-67); 401-233

Highest Field Goal Pct – Season (minimum 14 attempts)
92.86 Matt Stover (1994); 28-26
90.63 Matt Stover (1995); 32-29
88.46 Lou Groza (1953); 26-23
87.50 Matt Bahr (1983); 24-21
87.50 Don Cockroft (1974); 16-14

Most Safeties – Career
2 Walter Johnson (1965-76)

Most Safeties – Season
1 by 11 players; most recent Anthony Pleasant (1993)

RUSHING

Most Rushing Attempts - Career
2,359 Jim Brown (1957-65)
1,727 Leroy Kelly (1964-73)
1,593 Mike Pruitt (1976-84)
1,291 Kevin Mack (1985-93)
1,158 Greg Pruitt (1973-81)

Most Rushing Attempts - Season
305 Jim Brown (1961)
293 Mike Pruitt (1983)
291 Jim Brown (1963)
290 Jim Brown (1959)
289 Jim Brown (1965)

Most Rushing Attempts - Game
37 Jim Brown (10/04/1959 at Chicago Cardinals)
34 Jim Brown (11/19/1961 vs. Philadelphia Eagles)
34 Jim Brown (10/12/1958 vs. Chicago Cardinals)
33 Jim Brown (12/13/1959 at Philadelphia Eagles)
32 Larry Mason (10/04/1987 at New England Patriots)
32 Mike Pruitt (12/03/1981 at Houston Oilers)
32 Jim Brown (11/01/1959 at Baltimore Colts)

Most Rushing Yards - Career
12,312 Jim Brown (1957-65)
7,274 Leroy Kelly (1964-73)
6,540 Mike Pruitt (1976-84)
5,496 Greg Pruitt (1973-81)
5,123 Kevin Mack (1985-93)

Most Rushing Yards - Season
1,863 Jim Brown (1963)
1,544 Jim Brown (1965)
1,527 Jim Brown (1958)
1,446 Jim Brown (1964)
1,408 Jim Brown (1961)

Most Rushing Yards - Game
237 Jim Brown (11/19/1961 vs. Philadelphia Eagles)
237 Jim Brown (11/24/1957 vs. Los Angeles Rams)
232 Jim Brown (09/22/1963 at Dallas Cowboys)
232 Bobby Mitchell (11/15/1959 at Washington Redskins)
223 Jim Brown (11/03/1963 at Philadelphia Eagles)
214 Greg Pruitt (12/14/1975 vs. Kansas City Chiefs)
191 Greg Pruitt (10/17/1976 at Atlanta Falcons)

188 Earnest Byner (12/16/1984 at Houston Oilers)
188 Jim Brown (10/18/1964 at Dallas Cowboys)
188 Marion Motley (10/29/1950 vs. Pittsburgh Steelers)

Most Seasons 1,000 or More Yards Rushing
7 Jim Brown (1958-61, 63-65)
8 Mike Pruitt (1979-81, 83)

Most Games 100 or More Yards Rushing – Career
58 Jim Brown (1957-65)

Most Games 100 or More Yards Rushing – Season
7 Jim Brown (1958, 63)

Most Consecutive 100-Yard Rushing Games
6 Jim Brown (1958)
5 Jim Brown (1961)

Most Rushing TDs - Career
106 Jim Brown (1957-65)
74 Leroy Kelly (1964-73)
47 Mike Pruitt (1976-84)
46 Kevin Mack (1985-93)
33 Otto Graham (1950-55)

Most Rushing TDs - Season
17 Jim Brown (1965)
17 Jim Brown (1958)
16 Leroy Kelly (1968)
15 Leroy Kelly (1966)
14 Jim Brown (1959)

Most Rushing TDs - Game
5 Jim Brown (11/01/1959 at Baltimore Colts)
4 Leroy Kelly (12/01/1968 vs. New York Giants)
4 Jim Brown (11/18/1962 vs. St. Louis Cardinals)
4 Jim Brown (11/19/1961 vs. Philadelphia Eagles)
4 Jim Brown (10/26/1958 at Chicago Cardinals)
4 Jim Brown (11/24/1957 vs. Los Angeles Rams)
4 Dub Jones (11/25/1951 vs. Chicago Bears)

Most Consecutive Games with Rushing TD
7 Leroy Kelly (1968)
7 Jim Brown (1957) 1 (1958) 6 and (1962) 2 (1963) 5

Best Rushing Average - Career (minimum 500 attempts)
5.22 Jim Brown (1957-65); 2,359-12,312
4.80 Ernie Green (1962-68); 668-3,204
4.75 Greg Pruitt (1973-81); 1,158-5,496
4.21 Leroy Kelly (1964-73); 1,727-7,274
4.19 Cleo Miller (1975-82); 546-2,286

Best Rushing Average - Season (minimum 150 attempts)
6.40 Jim Brown (1963); 291-1,863
5.94 Jim Brown (1958); 257-1,527
5.85 Jim Brown (1960); 215-1,257
5.46 Leroy Kelly (1966); 209-1,141
5.45 Greg Pruitt (1978); 176-960

Best Rushing Average - Game (minimum 11 attempts)
17.09 Marion Motley (10/29/1950 vs. Pittsburgh Steelers); 11-188
16.57 Bobby Mitchell (11/15/1959 at Washington Redskins); 14-232
13.36 Bobby Mitchell (10/12/1959 vs. Chicago Cardinals); 11-147
11.67 Bobby Mitchell (12/03/1961 at Dallas Cowboys); 12-140
11.60 Jim Brown (09/22/1963 at Dallas Cowboys); 20-232

PASSING

Most Pass Attempts – Career
3,439 Brian Sipe (1973-83)
3,150 Bernie Kosar (1985-93)
1,755 Frank Ryan (1962-68)
1,565 Otto Graham (1950-55)
1,317 Mike Phipps (1970-76)

Most Pass Attempts - Season
567 Brian Sipe (1981)
554 Brian Sipe (1980)
535 Brian Sipe (1979)
531 Bernie Kosar (1986)
513 Bernie Kosar (1989)

Most Pass Attempts - Game
57 Brian Sipe (09/07/1981 vs. San Diego Chargers)
54 Eric Zeier (11/05/1995 vs. Houston Oilers)
53 Brian Sipe (09/13/1981 vs. Houston Oilers)
50 Bernie Kosar (11/10/1986 vs. Miami Dolphins)
49 Bernie Kosar (12/22/1991 at Pittsburgh Steelers)
49 Brian Sipe (10/16/1983 at Pittsburgh Steelers)
49 Otto Graham (10/04/1952 at Pittsburgh Steelers)

Most Pass Completions - Career
1,944 Brian Sipe (1973-83)
1,853 Bernie Kosar (1985-93)
907 Frank Ryan (1962-68)
872 Otto Graham (1950-55)
689 Bill Nelsen (1968-72)

Most Pass Completions - Season
337 Brian Sipe (1980)
313 Brian Sipe (1981)
310 Bernie Kosar (1986)
307 Bernie Kosar (1991)
303 Bernie Kosar (1989)

Most Pass Completions - Game
33 Brian Sipe (12/05/1982 vs. San Diego Chargers)
32 Bernie Kosar (11/10/1986 vs. Miami Dolphins)
31 Brian Sipe (09/07/1981 vs. San Diego Chargers)
30 Brian Sipe (10/25/1981 vs. Baltimore Colts)
30 Brian Sipe (12/07/1980 vs. New York Jets)

Highest Completion Pct - Career (minimum 750 attempts)
58.83 Bernie Kosar (1985-93); 3,150-1,853
57.89 Milt Plum (1957-61); 1,083-627

57.59 Vinny Testaverde (1993-95); 969-558
56.53 Brian Sipe (1973-83); 3,439-1,944
55.72 Otto Graham (1950-55); 1,565-872

**Highest Completion Pct - Season
(minimum 200 attempts)**
64.73 Otto Graham (1953); 258-167
62.15 Bernie Kosar (1991); 494-307
61.95 Bernie Kosar (1987); 389-241
60.88 Vinny Testaverde (1995); 363-221
60.83 Brian Sipe (1980); 554-337

**Highest Completion Pct - Game
(minimum 15 attempts)**
91.30 Vinny Testaverde (12/26/1993 at Los
    Angeles Rams); 23-21
82.61 Bernie Kosar (12/06/1992 vs.
    Cincinnati Bengals); 23-19
82.35 George Ratterman (10/06/1956 at
    Pittsburgh Steelers); 17-14
82.14 Brian Sipe (10/24/1976 vs. San Diego
    Chargers); 28-23
81.82 Bernie Kosar (11/05/1989 at Tampa
    Bay Buccaneers); 22-18

Most Consecutive Pass Completions
16 Bernie Kosar (10-29-89 vs. Hou.
    through 11-5-89 at T. B.)
15 Vinny Testaverde (12-26-93 at Rams
    through 1-2-94 at Pitt.)
14 Brian Sipe (12-5-82 vs. S.D.)
13 Paul McDonald (10-28-84 vs. N.O.)
13 Brian Sipe (9-28-80 vs. T.B.)

Most Passing Yards - Career
23,713 Brian Sipe (1973-83)
21,904 Bernie Kosar (1985-93)
13,499 Otto Graham (1950-55)
13,361 Frank Ryan (1962-68)
9,725 Bill Nelsen (1968-72)

Most Passing Yards - Season
4,132 Brian Sipe (1980)
3,876 Brian Sipe (1981)
3,854 Bernie Kosar (1986)
3,793 Brian Sipe (1979)
3,566 Brian Sipe (1983)

Most Passing Yards - Game
444 Brian Sipe (10/25/1981 vs. Baltimore
    Colts)
414 Bernie Kosar (11/23/1986 vs. Pitts-
    burgh Steelers)
401 Bernie Kosar (11/10/1986 vs. Miami
    Dolphins)
401 Otto Graham (10/04/1952 at Pitts-
    burgh Steelers)
391 Brian Sipe (10/19/1980 vs. Green Bay
    Packers)
375 Brian Sipe (09/07/1981 vs. San Diego
    Chargers)
369 Otto Graham (10/15/1950 vs. Chicago
    Cardinals)
367 Frank Ryan (12/17/1966 at St. Louis
    Cardinals)
358 Brian Sipe (11/18/1979 vs. Miami
    Dolphins)
353 Bernie Kosar (12/10/1989 at India-
    napolis Colts)

Most Passing TDs - Career
154 Brian Sipe (1973-83)
134 Frank Ryan (1962-68)
116 Bernie Kosar (1985-93)
88 Otto Graham (1950-55)
71 Bill Nelsen (1968-72)

Most Passing TDs - Season
30 Brian Sipe (1980)
29 Frank Ryan (1966)
28 Brian Sipe (1979)
26 Brian Sipe (1983)
25 Frank Ryan (1964)
25 Frank Ryan (1963)

Most Passing TDs - Game
5 Brian Sipe (10/07/1979 vs. Pittsburgh
    Steelers)
5 Bill Nelsen (11/02/1969 vs. Dallas
    Cowboys)
5 Frank Ryan (12/12/1964 at New York
    Giants)

Most Consecutive Games TD Pass
23 Frank Ryan (1965) 1 (1967) 8
18 Milt Plum (1959) 1 (1961) 5

**Highest QB Rating - Career (minimum
750 attempts)**
89.93 Milt Plum (1957-61)
81.64 Bernie Kosar (1985-93)
81.43 Frank Ryan (1962-68)
80.18 Vinny Testaverde (1993-95)
78.17 Otto Graham (1950-55)

**Highest QB Rating - Season (minimum
200 attempts)**
110.37 Milt Plum (1960)
99.66 Otto Graham (1953)
95.41 Bernie Kosar (1987)
91.37 Brian Sipe (1980)
90.59 Frank Ryan (1963)

**Highest QB Rating - Game (minimum
15 attempts)**
158.33 Brian Sipe (10/29/1978 vs. Buffalo
    Bills)
158.33 Otto Graham (10/10/1954 vs.
    Chicago Cardinals)
154.86 Milt Plum (11/13/1960 vs. St. Louis
    Cardinals)
153.94 Milt Plum (10/25/1959 vs.
    Washington Redskins)
150.57 Brian Sipe (11/19/1978 at Baltimore
    Colts)

Most Passes Intercepted - Career
149 Brian Sipe (1973-83)
94 Otto Graham (1950-55)
88 Frank Ryan (1962-68)
81 Mike Phipps (1970-76)
81 Bernie Kosar (1985-93)

Most Passes Intercepted - Season
26 Brian Sipe (1979)
25 Brian Sipe (1981)
24 Otto Graham (1952)
23 Paul McDonald (1984)
23 Brian Sipe (1983)
23 Bill Nelsen (1971)

Most Passes Intercepted - Game
6 Brian Sipe (10/16/1983 at Pittsburgh
    Steelers)
6 Brian Sipe (11/22/1981 vs. Pittsburgh
    Steelers)
5 Frank Ryan (11/06/1966 at Pittsburgh
    Steelers)
5 Otto Graham (10/17/1954 at Pittsburgh
    Steelers)

**Most Consecutive Attempts Without
an Interception**
308* Bernie Kosar (1990-91)
208 Milt Plum (1959-60)

**Lowest Interception Pct - Career
(minimum 750 attempts)**
2.57 Bernie Kosar (1985-93); 3,150-1,853
3.60 Milt Plum (1957-61); 1,083-627
3.72 Vinny Testaverde (1993-95); 969-558
4.33 Brian Sipe (1973-83); 3,439-1,944
4.82 Paul McDonald (1980-85); 767-411

**Lowest Interception Pct - Season
(minimum 200 attempts)**
1.82 Bernie Kosar (1991); 494-307
1.88 Bernie Kosar (1986); 531-310
2.00 Milt Plum (1960); 250-151
2.31 Bernie Kosar (1987); 389-241
2.48 Vinny Testaverde (1995); 363-221

RECEIVING

Most Receptions - Career
662 Ozzie Newsome (1978-90)
331 Gary Collins (1962-71)
323 Greg Pruitt (1973-81)
315 Brian Brennan (1984-91)
310 Reggie Rucker (1975-81)

Most Receptions - Season
89 Ozzie Newsome (1984)
89 Ozzie Newsome (1983)
69 Ozzie Newsome (1981)
65 Webster Slaughter (1989)
65 Greg Pruitt (1981)

Most Receptions - Game
14 Ozzie Newsome (10/14/1984 vs. New
    York Jets)
11 Webster Slaughter (12/22/1991 at
    Pittsburgh Steelers)
11 Mac Speedie (11/09/1952 vs. Chicago
    Cardinals)

**Most Consecutive Games with
Reception**
150 Ozzie Newsome (1979) 9 (1989) 7
53 Mike Pruitt (1979) 7 (1983) 5

Most Receiving Yards - Career
7,980 Ozzie Newsome (1978-90)
5,508 Ray Renfro (1952-63)
5,299 Gary Collins (1962-71)
5,210 Paul Warfield (1964-69,1976-77)
4,953 Reggie Rucker (1975-81)

Most Receiving Yards - Season
1,236 Webster Slaughter (1989)
1,067 Paul Warfield (1968)
1,002 Ozzie Newsome (1981)
1,001 Ozzie Newsome (1984)
982 Dave Logan (1979)

Most Receiving Yards - Game
191 Ozzie Newsome (10/14/1984 vs. New
    York Jets)
186 Webster Slaughter (10/23/1989 vs.
    Chicago Bears)
184 Webster Slaughter (10/29/1989 vs.
    Houston Oilers)
182 Darrell Brewster (12/06/1953 vs. New
    York Giants)
177 Eric Metcalf (09/20/1992 at Los
    Angeles Raiders)
177 Reggie Rucker (11/18/1979 vs. Miami

Dolphins)
177 Gern Nagler (11/20/1960 at Pittsburgh Steelers)
176 Brian Brennan (12/21/1986 vs. San Diego Chargers)
173 Andre Rison (10/29/1995 at Cincinnati Bengals)
171 Derrick Alexander (12/04/1994 vs. New York Giants)

Most Seasons 50 or More Receptions
6 Ozzie Newsome (1979-81, 83-85)
7 Gary Collins (1965-66, 69)
8 Webster Slaughter (1989-91)
3 Eric Metcalf (1989-90, 93)

Highest Receiving Average - Career (minimum 100 receptions)
19.60 Ray Renfro (1952-63); 281-5,508
19.23 Paul Warfield (1964-69,1976-77); 271-5,210
18.44 Ricky Feacher (1976-84); 113-2,084

Highest Receiving Average - Season (minimum 20 receptions)
28.05 Ray Renfro (1957); 21-589
23.88 Ray Renfro (1958); 24-573
22.55 Ricky Feacher (1981); 29-654

Highest Receiving Average - Game (minimum 3 receptions)
52.33 Rich Kreitling (10/02/1960 vs. Pittsburgh Steelers); 3-157
48.67 Clarence Weathers (10/13/1985 at Houston Oilers); 3-146
46.00 Webster Slaughter (10/29/1989 vs. Houston Oilers); 4-184

Most Receiving TDs - Career
70 Gary Collins (1962-71)
52 Paul Warfield (1964-69,1976-77)
50 Ray Renfro (1952-63)
47 Ozzie Newsome (1978-90)
33 Dante Lavelli (1950-56)

Most Receiving TDs - Season
13 Gary Collins (1963)
12 Paul Warfield (1968)
12 Gary Collins (1966)
11 Gary Collins (1969)
10 Paul Warfield (1969)
10 Gary Collins (1965)

Most Receiving TDs - Game
3 Eric Metcalf (09/20/1992 at Los Angeles Raiders)
3 Calvin Hill (11/19/1978 at Baltimore Colts)
3 Larry Poole (11/13/1977 at Pittsburgh Steelers)
3 Reggie Rucker (09/12/1976 vs. New York Jets)
3 Gary Collins (10/20/1963 vs. Philadelphia Eagles)
3 Ray Renfro (11/22/1959 vs. Pittsburgh Steelers)
3 Darrell Brewster (12/06/1953 vs. New York Giants)
3 Mac Speedie (12/02/1951 vs. Chicago Cardinals)

Most Consecutive Games with TD Reception
6 Gary Collins (1963) 2 (1964) 5
6 Paul Warfield (1968)

INTERCEPTIONS
Most Passes Intercepted - Career
45 Thom Darden (1972-74,1976-81)
40 Warren Lahr (1950-59)
39 Clarence Scott (1971-83)
30 Ken Konz (1953-59)
29 Bernie Parrish (1959-66)

Most Passes Intercepted - Season
10 Thom Darden (1978)
9 Eric Turner (1994)
9 Felix Wright (1989)
9 Tommy James (1950)

Most Passes Intercepted - Game
3 Stevon Moore (09/17/1995 at Houston Oilers)
3 Frank Minnifield (11/22/1987 at Houston Oilers)
3 Hanford Dixon (12/19/1982 vs. Pittsburgh Steelers)
3 Ron Bolton (11/27/1977 vs. Los Angeles Rams)
3 Ross Fichtner (10/23/1966 vs. Dallas Cowboys)
3 Bernie Parrish (12/03/1961 at Dallas Cowboys)
3 Bobby Franklin (12/11/1960 vs. Chicago Bears)
3 Tommy James (11/01/1953 vs. Washington Redskins)
3 Tommy James (11/05/1950 at Chicago Cardinals)

Most TDs on Interceptions - Career)
5 Warren Lahr (1950-59)
4 Ken Konz (1953-59)
3 Bernie Parrish (1959-66)
3 Jim Houston (1960-72)
3 Ross Fichtner (1960-67)
3 Erich Barnes (1965-71)

Most TDs on Interceptions - Season
2 Thane Gash (1989)
2 Jim Houston (1967)
2 Bobby Franklin (1960)
2 Ken Konz (1954)
2 Warren Lahr (1951)
2 Warren Lahr (1950)

Most TDs on Interceptions - Game
2 Bobby Franklin (12/11/1960 vs. Chicago Bears)

PUNTING
Most Punts - Career
651 Don Cockroft (1968-80)
385 Horace Gillom (1950-56)
336 Gary Collins (1962-71)
253 Jeff Gossett (1983,1985-87)
236 Brian Hansen (1991-93)

Most Punts - Season
97 Bryan Wagner (1989)
90 Don Cockroft (1974)
83 Jeff Gossett (1986)
82 Brian Hansen (1993)
82 Don Cockroft (1975)
82 Don Cockroft (1973)

Most Punts - Game
12 Bryan Wagner (11/19/1989 vs. Kansas City Chiefs)

12 Horace Gillom (12/03/1950 vs. Philadelphia Eagles)
11 Don Cockroft (10/15/1972 vs. Chicago Bears)
11 Gary Collins (12/12/1965 at Los Angeles Rams)
11 Horace Gillom (10/04/1953 at Chicago Cardinals)

Most Punt Yards - Career
26,262 Don Cockroft (1968-80)
16,872 Horace Gillom (1950-56)
13,764 Gary Collins (1962-71)
10,317 Jeff Gossett (1983,1985-87)
10,112 Brian Hansen (1991-93)

Most Punt Yards - Season
3,817 Bryan Wagner (1989)
3,643 Don Cockroft (1974)
3,632 Brian Hansen (1993)
3,498 Don Cockroft (1972)
3,423 Jeff Gossett (1986)

Most Punt Yards - Game
510 Horace Gillom (12/03/1950 vs. Philadelphia Eagles)
497 Gary Collins (12/12/1965 at Los Angeles Rams)
480 Don Cockroft (10/15/1972 vs. Chicago Bears)
468 Horace Gillom (10/04/1953 at Chicago Cardinals)
463 Bryan Wagner (11/19/1989 vs. Kansas City Chiefs)

Best Gross Punting Average - Career (minimum 50 attempts)
43.82 Horace Gillom (1950-56); 385-16,872
42.85 Brian Hansen (1991-93); 236-10,112
42.64 Sam Baker (1960-61); 108-4,605
42.02 Steve Cox (1981-84); 190-7,984
41.69 Tom Tupa (1993-95); 139-5,795

Best Gross Punting Average - Season (minimum 35 attempts)
46.69 Gary Collins (1965); 65-3,035
45.69 Horace Gillom (1952); 61-2,787
45.49 Horace Gillom (1951); 73-3,321
44.29 Brian Hansen (1993); 82-3,632
43.81 Horace Gillom (1953); 63-2,760

Best Gross Punting Average - Game
58.00 Johnny Evans (12/03/1978 at Seattle Seahawks); 1-58
56.50 Sam Baker (11/13/1960 vs. St. Louis Cardinals); 2-113
54.75 Horace Gillom (11/28/1954 at New York Giants); 4-219
54.33 Gary Collins (10/17/1965 vs. Dallas Cowboys); 6-326
54.00 Dave Mays (09/26/1976 at Denver Broncos); 1-54

Most Punts Inside 20 YDL - Career
63 Brian Hansen (1991-93)
59 Jeff Gossett (1983,1985-87)
45 Bryan Wagner (1989-90)
43 Tom Tupa (1993-95)
38 Steve Cox (1981-84)

Most Punts Inside 20 YDL - Season
32 Bryan Wagner (1989)
28 Brian Hansen (1992)
27 Tom Tupa (1994)
21 Jeff Gossett (1986)
21 Greg Coleman (1977)

PUNT RETURNS

Most Punt Returns - Career
161 Gerald McNeil (1986-89)
127 Eric Metcalf (1989-94)
111 Dino Hall (1979-83)
94 Leroy Kelly (1964-73)
78 Keith Wright (1978-80)

Most Punt Returns - Season
49 Gerald McNeil (1989)
44 Eric Metcalf (1992)
40 Gerald McNeil (1986)
39 Dino Hall (1983)
38 Gerald McNeil (1988)

Most Punt Returns - Game
7 Eric Metcalf (11/08/1992 at Houston Oilers)
7 Gerald McNeil (11/19/1989 vs. Kansas City Chiefs)
7 Gerald McNeil (11/16/1986 at Los Angeles Raiders)
7 Gerald McNeil (10/12/1986 vs. Kansas City Chiefs)
7 Dino Hall (10/25/1981 vs. Baltimore Colts)
7 Chet Hanulak (11/07/1954 vs. Washington Redskins)

Most Punt Return Yards - Career
1,545 Gerald McNeil (1986-89)
1,341 Eric Metcalf (1989-94)
990 Leroy Kelly (1964-73)
901 Dino Hall (1979-83)
659 Greg Pruitt (1973-81)

Most Punt Return Yards - Season
496 Gerald McNeil (1989)
464 Eric Metcalf (1993)
429 Eric Metcalf (1992)
386 Gerald McNeil (1987)
349 Greg Pruitt (1974)

Most Punt Return Yards - Game
166 Eric Metcalf (10/24/1993 vs. Pittsburgh Steelers)
115 Eric Metcalf (09/04/1994 at Cincinnati Bengals)
109 Leroy Kelly (11/28/1965 at Pittsburgh Steelers)
106 Gerald McNeil (09/28/1986 vs. Detroit Lions)
103 Gerald McNeil (12/10/1989 at Indianapolis Colts)

Most Punt Return TDs - Career
5 Eric Metcalf (1989-94)
3 Leroy Kelly (1964-73)
3 Bobby Mitchell (1958-61)

Most Punt Return TDs - Season
2 Eric Metcalf (1994)
2 Eric Metcalf (1993)
2 Leroy Kelly (1965)

Most Punt Return TDs - Game
2 Eric Metcalf (10/24/1993 vs. Pittsburgh Steelers)

Highest Punt Return Average – Career (minimum 50 returns)
11.77 Greg Pruitt (1973-81); 56-659
11.24 Bobby Mitchell (1958-61); 54-607
10.56 Eric Metcalf (1989-94); 127-1,341
10.53 Leroy Kelly (1964-73); 94-990
9.60 Gerald McNeil (1986-89); 161-1,545

Highest Punt Return Average - Season (minimum 15 returns)
15.59 Leroy Kelly (1965); 17-265
12.93 Greg Pruitt (1974); 27-349
12.89 Eric Metcalf (1993); 36-464
12.72 Ben Davis (1967); 18-229
11.35 Gerald McNeil (1987); 34-386

Highest Punt Return Average - Game (minimum 3 returns)
28.75 Eric Metcalf (09/04/1994 at Cincinnati Bengals); 4-115
27.67 Eric Metcalf (10/23/1994 vs. Cincinnati Bengals); 3-83
27.67 Bobby Mitchell (10/08/1961 vs. Washington Redskins); 3-83
27.33 Greg Pruitt (10/27/1974 vs. Denver Broncos); 3-82
27.25 Leroy Kelly (11/28/1965 at Pittsburgh Steelers); 4-109

KICKOFF RETURNS

Most Kickoff Returns - Career
151 Dino Hall (1979-83)
139 Eric Metcalf (1989-94)
87 Glen Young (1984-85,1987-88)
82 Randy Baldwin (1991-94)
76 Leroy Kelly (1964-73)

Most Kickoff Returns - Season
52 Eric Metcalf (1990)
50 Dino Hall (1979)
47 Gerald McNeil (1986)
36 Dino Hall (1981)
35 Glen Young (1985)

Most Kickoff Returns - Game
9 Dino Hall (10/07/1979 vs. Pittsburgh Steelers)
8 Dino Hall (11/25/1979 at Pittsburgh Steelers)
7 Dino Hall (11/29/1981 vs. Cincinnati Bengals)

Most Kickoff Return Yards - Career
3,185 Dino Hall (1979-83)
2,806 Eric Metcalf (1989-94)
2,079 Glen Young (1984-85,1987-88)
1,872 Randy Baldwin (1991-94)
1,784 Leroy Kelly (1964-73)

Most Kickoff Return TDs - Career
3 Bobby Mitchell (1958-61)
2 Eric Metcalf (1989-94)

Most Kickoff Return TDs - Season
2 Eric Metcalf (1990)

Most Kickoff Return TDs - Game
1. 1 11 times; most recent Randy Baldwin (09/04/1994 at Cincinnati Bengals)

Highest Kickoff Return Average – Career (minimum 50 returns)
26.26 Greg Pruitt (1973-81); 58-1,523
25.94 Walter Roberts (1964-66); 62-1,608
25.24 Keith Wright (1978-80); 70-1,767
25.00 Bobby Mitchell (1958-61); 62-1,550
24.35 Billy Lefear (1972-75); 60-1,461

Highest Kickoff Return Average - Season (minimum 12 returns)
31.69 Billy Lefear (1975); 13-412
29.50 Billy Reynolds (1954); 14-413
28.88 Bo Scott (1969); 25-722
28.31 Greg Pruitt (1973); 16-453
27.55 Greg Pruitt (1974); 22-606

QUARTERBACK SACKS

Most Sacks - Career
76.5 Clay Matthews (1978-93)
69 Jerry Sherk (1970-81)
58 Walter Johnson (1965-76)

Most Sacks – Season
14.5 Bill Glass (1965)
14 Jack Gregory (1970)
14 Reggie Camp (1984)

Most Sacks - Game
4 Jerry Sherk (11-14-76 vs. Phil.)
4 Mack Mitchell (11-20-77 vs. N.Y.G.)

Most Consecutive Games At Least One Sack
7 Bill Glass (1966)

Most Sack Yards - Career
568 Clay Matthews (1978-92)
547 Jerry Sherk (1970-81)

Most Sack Yards - Season
125.5 Reggie Camp (1984)

Most Sack Yards – Game
39 Reggie Camp (11 -25-84 vs. Houston)

Cleveland Browns Team Records

GAMES WON

Most Games Won, One Season (Including Postseason)
13 (1986)
12 (1994)
12 (1950)

Most Games Won - Regular Season
12 (1986)
11 (1994)
11 (1980)
11 (1965)
11 (1953)
11 (1951)

Most Consecutive Games Won, Start of Season
7 (1953)

Most Consecutive Home Games Won (Regular Season)
12 (1950-52)

Most Consecutive Road Games Won
7 (1951-52; 54-55; 71-72)

GAMES LOST

Most Games Lost, One Season
13 (1990)
11 (1995)
11 (1984)
11 (1981)
11 (1975)

Most Consecutive Games Lost
8 (1974-75)

Most Consecutive Games Lost, Start of Season
9 (1975)

Most Consecutive Games Lost, End of Season
5 (1981)

Most Consecutive Home Games Lost
6 (1990)

Most Consecutive Road Games Lost
11 (1974-76)

SCORING

Most Points - Season
415 (1964); 22 FG, 49 PAT, 50 TD
403 (1966); 9 FG, 52 PAT, 54 TD
394 (1968); 18 FG, 46 PAT, 49 TD
391 (1986); 26 FG, 43 PAT, 45 TD
390 (1987); 21 FG, 45 PAT, 47 TD

Most Points - Game
62 (11/07/1954 vs. Washington Redskins); 2 FG, 8 PAT, 8 TD
62 (12/06/1953 vs. New York Giants); 2 FG, 8 PAT, 8 TD
52 (12/12/1964 at New York Giants); 1 FG, 7 PAT, 7 TD
51 (09/10/1989 at Pittsburgh Steelers); 3 FG, 6 PAT, 6 TD
49 (12/04/1966 vs. New York Giants); 7 PAT, 7 TD
49 (10/30/1966 at Atlanta Falcons); 7 PAT, 7 TD
49 (10/19/1952 at Philadelphia Eagles); 7 PAT, 7 TD
49 (12/02/1951 vs. Chicago Cardinals); 7 PAT, 7 TD
30 (01/17/1988 at Denver Broncos)

Photo Credits

Volume I

Pages 2-3 — Roger Mastroianni
Page 4, 6-7 — Elizabeth Fulford Schiau
Pages 8-9 — Stephen S. Counsel
Page 10, 12-13 — Ron Kuntz
Page 14 — Stephen S. Counsel
Page 16 — Cleveland Browns
Page 17 — Cleveland Press Collection, Cleveland State University Archives
Page 18, 19 — Janine Exner
Page 20 — Elizabeth Fulford Schiau
Page 21 — Ron Kuntz
Page 22, 24 — Stephen S. Counsel
Page 25 — Ron Kuntz
Pages 26-27 — Roger Mastroianni
Page 28, 29 — John H. Reid III
Page 30 — Stephen S. Counsel
Page 31 — Ron Kuntz
Page 32, 34, 35, 36 — Janine Exner
Page 37 — Elizabeth Fulford Schiau
Pages 38-39 — Stephen S. Counsel
Page 40 — United Press
Page 43 — Cleveland Press Collection, Cleveland State University Archives
Page 44 — Ron Kuntz
Page 45 — Ron Kuntz and Topps
Pages 46-47 — Roger Mastroianni
Page 48 — Ron Kuntz
Page 49 — left, Cleveland Browns; right, John H. Reid III
Page 50 — Cleveland Press Collection, CSU Archives
Page 52 — Timothy Culek
Pages 54-55, 57, 58 — Ron Kuntz
Page 60 — John H. Reid III
Page 61 — Ron Kuntz
Page 62, 66, 69, 71, 72 — John H. Reid III
Page 74 — Roger Mastroianni
Page 76, 81 — John H. Reid III
Page 82 — Stephen S. Counsel
Page 86 — John H. Reid III
Page 88 — Elizabeth Fulford Schiau
Page 91 — Stephen S. Counsel
Page 92 — Elizabeth Fulford Schiau
Page 94, 95 — Stephen S. Counsel
Page 96 — Ron Kuntz
Page 97 — Janine Exner
Page 98, 101, 102, 103 — Stephen S. Counsel
Page 104 — top, Ron Kuntz; bottom, Stephen S. Counsel
Page 106 — John H. Reid III
Page 109 — Woodford Press
Page 110, 112 — Stephen S. Counsel
Page 113 — Ron Kuntz
Page 144 — Stephen S. Counsel
Page 116 — John H. Reid III
Pages 118, 119 — Janine Exner
Page 120, 122, 123, 124, 125, 126, 129, 130, 131 — Ron Kuntz
Page 133, 134, 135 — Stephen S. Counsel
Page 137 — Janine Exner
Page 138 — Stephen S. Counsel
Page 139 — Janine Exner
Page 140 — Roger Mastroianni
Page 141 — top, Janine Exner; bottom, Elizabeth Fulford Schiau
Page 142 — Janine Exner
Page 143 — Ron Kuntz

Page 144, 146, 147 148-149, 150 — Janine Exner
Page 152 — Ron Kuntz
Page 155 — Cleveland Browns
Page 156 — Cleveland Press Collection, CSU Archives
Page 158 — Cleveland Browns
Page 159 — Cleveland Press Collection, CSU Archives
Pages 160 and 161, 162 — Janine Exner
Page 162 — Janine Exner
Page 164 — Pro Football Hall of Fame
Page 166, 167 — Cleveland Press Collection, CSU Archives
Page 170 — H. G. Walker/*Life* magazine
Page 171 — Cleveland Press Collection, CSU Archives
Page 172 — Ron Kuntz
Page 192 — Janine Exner

Volume II

Page 2 — Ron Kuntz
Page 5 — Elizabeth Fulford Schiau
Pages 6 and 7 — Ron Kuntz
Page 8 — Roger Mastroianni
Page 10 — Ron Kuntz
Page 11 — Roger Mastroianni
Page 12 — Ron Kuntz
Page 14 — Elizabeth Fulford Schiau
Page 15 — Stephen S. Counsel
Pages 16 and 17 — Roger Mastroianni
Pages 18 and 19 — Stephen S. Counsel
Page 20 — Ron Kuntz
Page 22 — Ron Kuntz
Pages 23, 24 and 25, 26, 27 — Janine Exner
Page 28, 31 — Ron Kuntz
Pages 32 and 33 — Janine Exner
Pages 34-35, 36, 37 — Ron Kuntz
Page 38 — Janine Exner
Page 40 — Stephen S. Counsel
Page 41, 42 — Ron Kuntz
Page 43, 44 — Janine Exner
Page 45 — Stephen S. Counsel
Page 46 — Janine Exner
Page 47, 48, 50, 51, 52 — Ron Kuntz
Pages 55 — Elizabeth Fulford Schiau
Pages 56 — Janine Exner
Page 58, 60 — Ron Kuntz
Page 61 — Mort Tucker
Page 62 — Ron Kuntz
Page 64 — John H. Reid III
Page 67 — Ron Kuntz
Page 68 — Elizabeth Fulford Schiau
Pages 70-71 — Ron Kuntz
Page 72 — Stephen S. Counsel
Page 73 — John H. Reid III
Page 74 — Elizabeth Fulford Schiau
Page 75 — Ron Kuntz
Page 76 — Stephen S. Counsel
Pages 78-79 — Roger Mastroianni
Page 81 — Ron Kuntz
Page 82 — Stephen S. Counsel
Page 83, 84, 87, 89, 90 — Janine Exner
Pages 92-93 — Stephen S. Counsel
Page 95 — Janine Exner
Pages 96 — Roger Mastroianni

Acknowledgments

The Browns are back in time for the millennium. The new football stadium will be home and a showplace for years to come. And Cleveland has buffed up its shining national image.

Can-do Cleveland!

Leagues and franchises do not create need. People do. This two-volume books set exists as a history of one of the truly great comebacks in National Football League annals, but also as a tribute to a community spirit seldom seen.

Woodford Press is proud to publish these books — officially sanctioned by the Cleveland Browns. Our gratitude to the Browns and to their front-office staff is limitless. Namely Alex Martins, Bruce Popko

and Dan Arthur, a trio of all-pros when it comes to getting things done under pressure.

No shortage of all-stars on the Woodford staff as well. To name two: Tony "Encyclopedia" Khing and Anne "No Problem" Crump. Books like these take "24/7" commitments. The entire Woodford crew came through.

Special contributors also came up big — Clevelanders Rich Exner, associate editor on the project, and Ron Kuntz, chief photographer. The writers are well known to legions of Browns fans in Northern Ohio. And it is easy to see why book designer Tom Morgan enjoys a national reputation for brilliance.

Ah, but somebody had to make it all come together. We brought in Tim Graham to do that. And he did that, bringing his long experience as the editor of a daily newspaper and editor of a weekly high-tech magazine to the task. Did it help that Tim grew up in Ohio and has been a fiercely loyal Browns fan since birth? We think he was the only man for the job.

**DAVID BURGIN AND
DAN ROSS
Publishers
Woodford Press
November, 1999**

About the contributors

DAN COUGHLIN

Dan Coughlin is one of the most familiar names in Cleveland sports journalism, logging 35 years in the business, including the first 18 with *The* (Cleveland) *Plain Dealer*. He also worked for the *Cleveland Press* and United Press International. He currently stays busy as a sportscaster for Cleveland television station WJW and by writing syndicated sports columns for three suburban newspapers, the *Elyria Chronicle-Telegram*, the *Medina Gazette* and the *Lake County News Herald*. Dan and his wife, Maddy, have four children, Joe, John, Mike and Mary. They live in Rocky River, Ohio.

RON KUNTZ

Few, if any, photographers have covered more Cleveland sporting events during the last half-century than Ron Kuntz. But his work has also taken him abroad to photograph nine Olympic Games, other major sporting events and even exploration

at the South Pole. A pending assignment to cover the 2000 Olympics in Australia would place Ron on the lone continent where he has never covered news. Ron worked for United Press International and its predecessor, UP, in Cleveland from 1953 to 1991 before joining the Reuters news agency. Ron and his wife, Nancy, live in North Olmsted, Ohio. They have five children — Ronald, John, Stephen, Rebecca and Joshua — and five grandchildren.

TIM GRAHAM

Graham is editor-in-chief of *TechWeek*, a business and technology news magazine based in California's Silicon Valley, and previously was the editor of the *Oakland Tribune*. An Ohio native, Graham began his journalism career at the *Mount Vernon News* and later was a reporter for the *Cincinnati Post* and *Dayton Daily News*. He remains a part owner of the *Buckeye Sports Bulletin* in Columbus. He and his wife, Catherine Chriss,

have two daughters, Alison and Elizabeth, and live in Oakland, California.

RICH EXNER

Rich Exner has been with *The* (Cleveland) *Plain Dealer* since 1991, most recently working as a news reporter after starting at the newspaper as a sports copy editor. Previously, he was the Cleveland bureau manager and Ohio state editor for United Press International. Rich worked part-time as sportswriter for the *Wheeling* (West Virginia) *News-Register*, the *Wheeling Intelligencer*, the *Columbus Dispatch* and the *Buckeye Sports Bulletin* before graduating from Ohio State University with a journalism degree in 1987. He and his wife, Janine, have two sons, Dillon and Owen. They live in North Olmsted, Ohio.

STEVE HERRICK

Steve Herrick is a 20-year veteran of sports reporting, most recently working as a freelance writer for the

"Cleveland Live" site on the Internet, the *Sporting News* and various other publications. Steve was the Indians beat writer for the *Chronicle-Telegram* in Elyria, Ohio, from 1986 to 1997, and also covered the Browns and the Cavaliers for the newspaper. After graduating from Ohio University with a degree in journalism in 1979, Steve began his career at the *Parkersburg (West Virginia) News*. He and his wife, Linda, live in North Ridgeville, Ohio.

JANINE EXNER

Janine Exner has worked as a photographer in the Cleveland area since 1985. Most recently, she has done freelance work for the Associated Press. Previously, she worked for the *Chronicle-Telegram* in Elyria, Ohio, the *Wheeling (West Virginia) News-Register* and the *Wheeling Intelligencer*. Janine is a 1983 graduate of West Liberty State College in West Virginia with degrees in communications and business. She and her husband, Rich, have two sons, Dillon and Owen. They live in North Olmsted, Ohio.

ROGER MASTROIANNI

Roger Mastroianni has been shooting pictures professionally in Cleveland for 20 years, handling news assignments for a variety of outlets, including *Business Week*, *Forbes*, *Fortune*, *Newsweek*, *Rolling Stone*, the *New York Times* and United Press International. He has provided photography for a number of books and does publicity photography for Cleveland's professional theaters and the Cleveland Orchestra. Roger lives in Lyndhurst, Ohio with his wife, Barbara, and their children, Maxwell, Samson and Mia.

ELIZABETH FULFORD SCHIAU

Elizabeth Fulford Schiau has worked as a freelance photographer in Cleveland since 1988. Her work as included assignments from the Associated Press and Crain's *Cleveland Business*. Previously, she worked for *The Star-Ledger*, in Newark, New Jersey. Elizabeth is a 1985 graduate of Ohio University with a degree in photojournalism. She is married with two children and lives in Rocky River, Ohio.

STEPHEN S. COUNSEL

Stephen S. Counsel has worked for newspapers in Florida, Mississippi and Ohio since graduating from the University of South Florida with a degree in filmmaking in 1983. He has covered a variety of major sports events in Cleveland, including the 1997 baseball all-star game and the 1997 NBA all-star game, and has spent time working on a master's degree in photojournalism at Ohio University. Stephen and his wife, Laurie, and their son, Eric, live in Columbus, Ohio.

TOM MORGAN

Tom Morgan walks on water when it comes to designing books. His keen eye and artistic talent have enhanced both text and images for top-selling illustrated histories such as *The Martini* and *The Cigar*, by Barnaby Conrad III (Chronicle Books), and for art books such as Conrad's *John Register: Persistent Obvserver* (Woodford Press). He has authored two books, *Saints* (Chronicle Books) and *The Devil* (Chronicle Books). His design firm, Blue Design, is based in Portland, Maine, where he lives with his wife, Genevieve, and son, Graham.

Trivial pursuing

Here are the answers to the *Otto Who?* trivia quiz on pages 51-57.

1. Cliff Lewis of Lakewood.
2. Leroy Kelly, who finished his playing career in 1973, was inducted in 1994.
3, The Panthers.
4. Brian Sipe.
5. Bowling Green State University, from 1946-1951.
6. 46.
7. Chuck Noll, Mike Michalske and Tom Mack.
8. Paul Brown.
9. The Cardinals, Lions, Rams and Browns.
10. New York in 1946 and 1947, Buffalo in 1948 and San Francisco in 1949.
11. Tiny Tim.

12. The players are, in respective order, Carl Hairston, Hanford Dixon, Mike Golic, Clay Matthews, Kevin Mack, Earnest Byner, Mike Baab, Mike Pagel, Ozzie Newsome, Dan Fike, Scott Nicolas and Dave Puzzuoli.
13. Texas (24), Pennslvania (21) and Ohio (19). The only other states with at least 10 Hall of Famers are Illinois and California, with 12 each.
14. Chris Kelley from Lorain Catholic High School caught a pass on a botched extra point.
15. Thom Darden.
16. Todd Philcox.
17. Dave Jacobs.
18. Pitttsburgh Steelers.
19. Four times, in 1950, 1954, 1955 and 1964.
20. 5-3.
21. Mark Moseley, who was signed to finish the 1986 season after Matt Bahr was injured.
22. The Doak Walker Award. Walker was drafted by the Browns in 1949 but played that year for SMU His rights were traded to Detroit in 1950.
23. Milt Plum, the starting QB from 1958 through 1961.
24. Defensive back Jim Shofner.
25. John Havlicek, who went on to a Hall of Fame basketball career.
26. Clay Matthews.
27. Ohio State with 31, followed by Purdue with 22, Michigan State with 19, Michigan with 15, and Illinois and Baylor with 14 each.
28. They were the first black players to play professional football since 1933. Their debuts came eight months before Jackie Robinson broke baseball's color barrier.
29. Never. Groza played only three games on Ohio State's freshman team before entering the Army. When the war was over, he joined the Browns.
30. Yes. City voters in 1928 approved a $2.5 million bond issue to support construction of what was billed as the largest outdoor stadium in the world (78,189 seats).
31. Four, including the first three: Paul Brown, 167-53-8; Blanton Collier, 79-38-2; and Nick Skorich, 30-26-2. The only other Browns coach with a winning record was Marty Schottenheimer, 46-31.
32. Otto Graham.

All-time Browns roster

A

Abrams, Bobby (LB) Michigan 92

Adamle, Tony (FB) Ohio State 47-51, 54

Adams, Chet (T) Ohio 46-48

Adams, Pete (G) Southern California 74, 76

Adams, Stefon (DB) Auburn 90

Adams, Vashone (DB) Eastern Michigan 95

Adams, Willis (WR) Houston 79-85

Aeilts, Rick (TE) S.E. Miss State ##89

Agase, Alex (G) Illinois 48-51

Akins, Al (RB) Washington State 46

Aldridge, Allen (DE) Prairie View 74

Alexander, Derrick (WR) Michigan 94-95

Allen, Ermal (QB) Kentucky 47

Allen, Greg (RB) Florida State. 85

Alzado, Lyle (DE) Yankton 79-81

Ambrose, Dick (LB) Virginia 75-83

Amstutz, Joe (C) Indiana 57

Anderson, Herbie (DB) Texas A&I ##92

Anderson, Preston (DB) Rice 74

Anderson, Stuart (LB) Virginia 84

Andrews, Billy (LB) S.E. Louisiana 67-74

Arvie, Herman (OL) Grambling 95

Askin, John (G) Notre Dame *87

Athas, Pete (DB) Tennessee 75

Arvie, Herman (T) Grambling 93-94

Atkins, Doug (DE) Tennessee 53-54

B

Baab, Mike (C) Texas 82-87, 90-91

Babich, Bob (LB) Miami (Ohio) 73-78

Bahr, Matt (K) Penn State 81-89

Baker, Al (DE) Colorado State 87, 89-90

Baker, Sam (P-K) Oregon State 60-61

Baker, Tony (RB) East Carolina 86,88

Baldwin, Keith (DE) Texas A&M 82-85

Baldwin, Randy (RB) Mississippi #91-94

Ball, Jerry (DT) Southern Methodist 93

Bandison, Romeo (DL) Oregon #94-95

Banker, Ted (G) S.E. Mississippi St. 89

Banks, Carl (LB) Michigan State 94-95

Banks, Chip (LB) Southern California 82-86

Banks, Fred (WR) Liberty 85

Banks, Robert (DE) Notre Dame 89-90

Barisich, Carl (DT) Princeton 73-75

Barnes, Erich (DB) Purdue 65-71

Barnett, Harlon (S) Michigan State 90-92

Barnett, Vincent (S) Arkansas State *87

Barney, Eppie (WR) Iowa State 67-68

Bassett, Maurice (RB) Langston 54-56

Bates, Michael (WR/KR) Arizona 95

Battle, Jim (DE) Southern University 66

Baugh, Tom (C) Southern Illinois 89

Bavaro, Mark (TE) Notre Dame 92

Beach, Walter (DB) Central Michigan 63-66

Beamon, Autry (DB) East Texas State 80-81

Beauford, Clayton (WR) Auburn *87

Bedosky, Mike (OL) Missouri #94

Belk, Rocky (WR) Miami 83

Bell, Terry (WR) Indiana State *87

Benz, Larry (DB) Northwestern 63-65

Berry, Latin (DB) Oregon 91-92

Best, Greg (S) Kansas State 84

Bettridge, Ed (LB) Bowling Green 64

Beutler, Tom (LB) Toledo 70

Biedermann, Leo (T) California 78

Bishop, Harold (TE) Louisiana State 95

Black, James (RB) Akron 84

Blandin, Ernie (T) Tulane 46-47

Blaylock, Anthony (DB) Winston-Salem 88-91

Bloch, Ray (T) Ohio #81

Boedeker, Bill (DB) No College 47-49

Bolden, Leroy (RB) Michigan State 58-59

Bolden, Rickey (T) Southern Methodist 84-89

Bolton, Ron (DB) Norfolk State 76-82

Bolzan, Scott (T) Northern Illinois #85

Booth, Issac (DB) California 94-95

Borton, John (QB) Ohio State 57

Bosley, Keith (OT) Eastern Kentucky *87

Bostic, Keith (DB) Michigan 90

Bradley, Harold (G) Iowa 54-56

Bradley, Henry (DT) Alcorn State 79-82

Brady, Donny (DB) Wisconsin 95

Braggs, Stephen (DB) Texas 87-91

Brandon, David (LB) Memphis State 91-93

Brannon, Robert (DE) Arkansas (Fayetteville) *87

Braziel, Larry (CB) Southern California 82-85

Brennan, Brian (WR) Boston College 84-91

Brewer, Johnny (TE-LB) Mississippi 61-67

Brewster, Darrell (WR) Purdue 52-58

Briggs, Bob (DE) Heidelberg 71-73

Briggs, Greg (S)Tex. Southern ##93

Brockman, Lonnie (LB) West Virginia ##91

Brooks, Clifford (DB) Tennessee State 72-74

Brooks, James (RB) Auburn 92

Brown, Dean (DB) Fort Valley State 69

Brown, Eddie (DB) Tennessee 74-75

Brown, Jerome (DL) Mississippi State ##93

Brown, Jim (RB) Syracuse 57-65

Brown, John (T) Syracuse 62-66

Brown, John III (WR) Houston ##92

Brown, Ken (RB) No College 70-75

Brown, Orlando (T) South Carolina State 94-95

Brown, Preston (KR) Vanderbilt 84

Brown, Richard (LB) San Diego State 91-92

Brown, Stan (WR) Purdue 71

Brown, Terry (DB) Oklahoma State 76

Brown, Thomas (DE) Baylor 81, 83

Buben, Mark (DT) Tufts 82

Buchanan, Charles (DE) Tennessee State 88

Buczkowski, Bob (DL) Pittsburgh 90

Buddenberg, John (OL) Akron 89

Buehler, George (G) Stanford 78-79

Bumgardner, Rex (RB) West Virginia 50-52

Bundra, Mike (DT)Southern California 64

Burnett, Rob (DE) Syracuse 90-95

Burrell, Clinton (DB) Louisiana State 79-84

Burton, Leonard (OL) South Carolina #91

Butler, Dave (LB) Notre Dame *87

Butler, Ray (WR) Southern California #89

Byner, Earnest (RB) East Carolina 84-88, 94-95

C

Caldwell, Mike (LB) Middle Tennessee State 93-95

Caleb, Jamie (RB) Grambling 60, 65

Camp, Reggie (DE) California 83-87

Campbell, Milt (RB) Indiana 57

Capers, James (LB) Central Michigan *87

Carollo, Joe (T) Notre Dame 72-73

Carpenter, Ken (RB) Oregon State 50-53

Carpenter, Lew (RB) Arkansas 57-58

Carpenter, Preston (RB) Arkansas 56-59

Carraway, Stanley (WR) West Texas State *87

Carreker, Vince (DB) Cincinnati *87

Carrier, Mark (WR) Nicholls State 93-94

Carter, Alex (DE) Tennessee State *87

Carver, Dale (LB) Georgia 83

Cassady, Howard (RB) Ohio State 62

Catlin, Tom (LB) Oklahoma 53-54, 57-58

Caylor, Lowell (DB) Miami (Ohio) 64

Charlton, Clifford (LB) Florida 88-89

Cheroke, George (G) Ohio State 46

Childress, Freddie (T) Arkansas 92

Christensen, Jeff (QB) Eastern Illinois *87
Clancy, Sam (DE) Pittsburgh 85-88
Clark, Monte (T) Southern California 63-69
Clarke, Frank (WR) Colorado 57-59
Clarke, Leon (WR) Southern California 60-62
Clayborn, Raymond (CB) Texas 90-91
Cline, Ollie (RB) Ohio State 48
Cockroft, Don (K-P) Adams State 68-80
Cole, Emerson (RB) Toledo 50-52
Colella, Tom (P-DB) Canisius 46-48
Coleman, Greg (P) Florida A&M 77
Collins, Gary (WR-P) Maryland 62-71
Collins, Larry (RB) Texas A&I 78
Collins, Shawn (WR) Northern Arizona 92
Colo, Don (T) Brown 53-58
Conjar, Larry (RB) Notre Dame 67
Connolly, Ted (G) Tulsa 63
Conover, Frank (DL) Syracuse 91
Contz, Bill (T) Penn State 83-86
Cooks, Johnie (LB) Mississippi State 91
Cooper, Scott (DE) Kearney State *87
Copeland,Jim (G) Virginia 67-74
Coppage, Alton (DE) Oklahoma 46
Cornell, Bo (RB) Washington 71-72
Costello, Vince (LB) Ohio University 57-66
Cotton, Fest (DT) Dayton 72
Cotton, Marcus (LB) Southern California 90
Cousineau, Tom (LB) Ohio State 82-85
Cowan, Bob (RB) Indiana 47-48
Cowher, Bill (LB) North Carolina State 80-82
Cox, Arthur (TE) Texas South 91
Cox, Steve (P-K) Arkansas 81-84
Craig, Neal (DB) Fisk 75-76
Craig, Reggie (WR) Arkansas 77
Craven, Bill (DB) Harvard 76
Crawford, Mike (RB) Arizona State *87
Crawford, Tim (LB) Texas Tech *87
Crespino, Bob (WR) Mississippi 61-63
Crews, Ron (DE) Nevada-Las Vegas 80
Crosby, Cleveland (DE) Arizona #80
Cureton, Will (QB) East Texas State 75
Cvercko, Andy (G) Northwestern 63

D

Dahl, Bob (OL) Notre Dame 92-95
Daniell, Jim (C) Ohio State 46
Danielson, Gary (QB) Purdue 85, 87-88
Darden, Thom (DB) Michigan 72-74, 76-81
Dark, Steve (TE) Middle Tennessee State ##93
Darrow,Barry (T) Montana 74-78
Davis, Ben (DB) Defiance 67-68, 70-73

Davis, Bruce (WR) Baylor 84
Davis, Dick (RB) Nebraska 69
Davis, Gary (RB) Cal Poly-SLO #81
Davis, Johnny (RB) Alabama 82-86, *87
Davis, Michael (CB) Cincinnati 95
Davis, Oliver (DB) Tennessee State 77-80
Davis, Willie (DE) Grambling 58-59
Dawson, Doug (G) Texas 94
Dawson, Len (QB) Purdue 60-61
DeLamielleure, Joe (G) Michigan State. 80-84
DeLeone, Tom (C) Ohio State 74-84
DeLeone, Tony (P) Kent State *87
Dellerba, Spiro (RB) Ohio State 47
DeMarco, Bob (C) Dayton 72-74
DeMarie, John (G-T) Louisiana State 67-75
Dennis, Al (G) Grambling 76-77
Dennison, Doug (RB) Kutztown State 79
Denton, Bob (DT) College of Pacific 60
Deschaine, Dick (DE) No College 58
Devries, Jed (OL) Utah State ##94, 95
Devrow, Billy (DB) Southern Mississippi 67
Dewar, Jim (RB) Indiana 47
Dickey, Curtis (RB) Texas A&M 85-86
Dieken, Doug (T) Illinois 71-84
Dimler, Rich (DT) Southern California 79
Dixon, Gerald (LB) South Carolina 93-95
Dixon, Hanford (CB) Southern Mississippi 81-89
Donaldson, Gene (G) Kentucky 53
Douglas, Derrick (RB) Louisisana Tech 91
Dressel, Chris (TE) Stanford #88
Driver, Stacey (RB) Clemson *87
Dudley, Brian (S) Bethune Cookman *87
Dumont, Jim (LB) Rutgers 84
Dunbar, Jubilee (WR) Southern 74
Duncan, Brian (RB) Southern Methodist 76-77
Duncan, Ron (TE) Wittenberg 67

E

East, Ron (DE) Montana State 75
Eaton, Chad (DL) Washington State #95
Echols, Donnie (TE) Oklahoma State *87
Edwards, Earl (DT) Wichita 76-78
Elkins, Mike (QB) Wake Forest #91
Ellis, Ken (DB) Southern 77
Ellis, Ray (S) Ohio State 86-87
Engel, Steve (RB) Colorado 70
Ethridge, Ray (WR) Pasadena City #95
Evans, Fred (RB) Notre Dame 46
Evans, Johnny (QB-P) North Carolina State 78-80
Everett, Major (RB) Mississippi College 86, *87
Everitt, Steve (C) Michigan 93-95

F

Fairchild,Greg (G) Tulsa 78
Farren, Paul (T) Boston University 83-91
Feacher, Ricky (WR) Mississippi Valley 76-84
Fekete, Gene (RB) Ohio State 46
Ferguson, Charley (DE) Tennessee A&I 61
Ferguson, Vagas (RB) Notre Dame 83
Ferrell, Kerry (WR) Syracuse ##93
Fichtner, Ross (DB) Purdue 60-67
Figaro, Cedric (LB) Notre Dame 91-92
Fike, Dan (G) Florida 85-92
Fiss, Galen (LB) Kansas 56-66
Fleming, Don (DB) Florida 60-62
Flick, Tom (QB) Washington 84
Flint, Judson (DB) Memphis State 80-82
Florence, Anthony (DB) Bethune Cookman 91
Foggie, Fred (DB) Minnesota 92
Fontenot, Herman (RB) Louisiana State 85-88
Footman, Dan (DE) Florida State 93-95
Ford, Henry (RB) Pittsburgh 55
Ford, Len (DE) Michigan 50-57
Forester, Herschel (G) Southern Methodist 54-57
Fortune, Elliott (DL) Georgia Tech #95
Franklin, Bobby (DB) Mississippi 60-66
Francis, Jeff (QB) Tennessee 90, #92
Franco, Brian (K) Penn State *87
Franks, Elvis (DE) Morgan State 80-84
Frederick, Andy (T) New Mexico 82
Frederick, Mike (DE) Virginia 95
Freeman, Bob (QB) Auburn 57-58
Fullwood, Brent (RB) Auburn 90
Fulton, Dan (WR) Nebraska-Omaha 81-82
Furman, John (QB) Texas-El Paso 62

G

Gain, Bob (DT) Kentucky 52, 54-64
Gainer, Derrick (RB) Florida A&M ##89, 90
Galbraith, Scott (TE) UCLA 90-92
Garcia, Jim (DE) Purdue 65
Garlington, John (LB) Louisiana State 68-77
Gartner, Chris (K) Indiana 74
Gash,Thane (S) E. Tennessee State 88-90
Gatski, Frank (C) Marshall 46-56
Gaudio, Bob (G) Ohio State 47-49, 51
Gault, Don (QB) Hofstra 70
Gautt, Prentice (RB) Oklahoma 60
George,Tim (WR) Carson-Newman 74
Gibron, Abe (G) Purdue 50-56
Gibson, Tom (DE) Northern Arizona 89-90
Gillom, Horace (P-WR) Nevada 47-56

Gilmore, Corey (RB) San Diego State *87

Glass, Bill (DE) Baylor 62-68

Glass, Chip (TE) Florida State 69-73

Goad, Tim (DT) North Carolina 95

Goebel, Brad (QB) Baylor 92-94

Goins, Robert (S) Grambling *87

Golic, Bob (DT) Notre Dame 82-88

Goode, Don (LB) Kansas 80-81

Goosby, Tom (LB) Baldwin Wallace 63

Gorgal, Ken (DB) Purdue 50, 53-54

Goss, Don (DT) Southern Methodist 56

Gossett, Jeff (P) East Illinois 83, 85-87

Graf,Dave (LB) Penn State 75-79

Graham, Jeff (QB) Long Beach State ##89

Graham, Otto (QB) Northwestern 46-55

Grant, Wes (DE) UCLA 72

Graybill, Mike (OL) Boston University 89

Grayson, David (LB) Fresno State *87-90

Green, Boyce (RB) Carson-Newman 83-85

Green, David (RB) Edinboro State 82

Green, Ernie (RB) Louisville 62-68

Green, Ron (WR) North Dakota 67-68

Green, Van (DB) Shaw 73-76

Greenwood, Don (RB) Illinois 46-47

Greer, Terry (WR) Alabama State 86

Gregory, Jack (DE) Delta State 67-71, 79

Griffin, Don (CB) Middle Tennessee State 94-95

Grigg, Forrest (DT) Tulsa. 48-51

Griggs, Anthony (LB) Ohio State 86-88

Gross, Al (S) Arizona 83-87

Groves, George (G) Marquette 46

Groza, Lou (T-K) Ohio St. 46-59, 61-67

Gruber, Bob (OT) Pittsburgh 86

Guilbeau, Rusty (LB) McNeese State *87

H

Hairston, Carl (DE) Maryland–East Shore 84-89

Hairston, Stacey (DB) Ohio Northern 93-94

Haley, Darryl (OL) Utah *87-88

Hall, Charlie (LB) Houston 71-80

Hall, Dana (S) Washington 95

Hall, Dino (KR-RB) Glassboro State 79-83

Haller, Alan (DB) Michigan State 92

Hannemann, Cliff (LB) Fresno State *87

Hanulak, Chet (RB) Maryland 54, 57

Hansen, Brian (P) Sioux Falls 91-93

Harper, Mark (CB) Alcorn State 86-90

Harraway, Charley (RB) San Jose State 66-68

Harrington, John (DE) Marquette 46

Harris, Duriel (WR) New Mexico State 4

Harris, Marshall (DE) Texas Christian 80-82

Harris, Odie (DB) Sam Houston State 91-92

Hartley, Frank (TE) Illinois 94-95

Harvey, Frank (FB) Georgia ##94

Haynes, Hayward (OL) Florida State ##91

Hawkins, Ben (WR) Arizona State 74

Helluin, Jerry (DT) Tulane 52-53

Herring, Hal (LB) Auburn 50-52

Hickerson, Gene (G) Mississippi 58-60, 62-73

Hilgenberg, Jay (C) Iowa 92

Hill, Calvin (RB) Yale 78-81

Hill, Jim (DB) Texas A&I 75

Hill, Travis (LB) Nebraska 94-95

Hill, Will (S) Bishop College 88

Hilliard, Randy (CB) Louisiana State 90-93

Hoaglin, Fred (C) Pittsburgh 66-72

Hoard, Leroy (RB) Michigan 90-95

Hoggard, D.D. (CB) North Carolina State 85-87

Holden, Steve (WR) Arizona State 73-76

Holland, Jamie (WR) Ohio State 92

Holloway, Glen (G) North Texas State 74

Holohan, Pete (TE) Notre Dame 92

Holt, Harry (TE) Arizona 83-86

Hooker, Fair (WR) Arizona State 69-74

Hoover, Houston (G) Jackson State 93

Hopkins, Thomas (T) Alabama A&M 83

Horn, Alvin (DB) Nevada–Las Vegas *87

Horn, Don (QB) San Diego State 73

Horvath, Les (RB) Ohio State 49

Houston, Jim (DE-LB) Ohio State 60-72

Houston, Lin (G) Ohio State 46-53

Howard, Sherman (RB) Nevada 52-53

Howell, Mike (DB) Grambling 65-72

Howton, Bill (WR) Rice 59

Humble, Weldon (LB) Rice 47-50

Hunt, Bob (RB) Heidelberg 74

Hunter, Art (C) Notre Dame 56-59

Hunter, Earnest (RB) Southeast Oklahoma State 95

Hutchinson, Tom (WR) Kentucky 63-65

Hutchison, Chuck (G) Ohio State 73-75

Huther, Bruce (LB) New Hampshire 81

Hynoski, Henry (RB) Temple 75

I

Ilgenfritz, Mark (DE)Vanderbilt 74

Ingram, Darryl (TE) California 91

Irons, Gerald (LB) Maryland–East Shore 76-79

Isaia, Sale (OL) UCLA #95

Isbell, Joe Bob (G) Houston 66

J

Jackson, Alfred (DB) San Diego State 91-92

Jackson, Bill (S) North Carolina 82

Jackson, Enis (CB) Memphis State *87

Jackson, Michael (WR) Southern Mississippi 91-95

Jackson, Rich (DE) Southern 72

Jackson, Robert E. (G) Duke 75-85

Jackson, Robert L. (LB) Texas A&M 78-81

Jacobs, Dave (K) Syracuse 81

Jacobs, Tim (CB) Delaware 93-95

Jaeger, Jeff (K) Washington 87

Jagade, Harry (RB) Indiana 51-53

James, Lynn (WR) Arizona State 91

James, Nathaniel (DB) Florida A&M 68

James, Tommy (DB) Ohio State 48-55

Jefferson, Ben (T) Maryland ##89, 90

Jefferson, John (WR) Arizona State 85

Jenkins, Al (G) Tulsa 69-70

Johnson, Bill (DL) Michigan State 92-94

Johnson, Eddie (LB) Louisville 81-90

Johnson, Lawrence (DB) Wisconsin 79-84

Johnson, Lee (P) Brigham Young 87-88

Johnson, Mark (LB) Missouri 77

Johnson, Mike (LB) Virginia Tech 86-93

Johnson, Mitch (T) UCLA 71

Johnson, Pepper (LB) Ohio State 93-95

Johnson, Ron (RB) Michigan 69

Johnson, Walter (DT) California State (Los Angeles) 65-76

Joines, Vernon (WR) Maryland 89-90

Jones, Bobby (WR) No College 83

Jones, Dave (WR) Kansas State 69-71

Jones, Dub (WR) Tulane 48-55

Jones, Edgar (RB) Pittsburgh 46-49

Jones, Homer (WR) Texas Southern 70

Jones, James (DL) Northern Iowa 91-94

Jones, Jock (LB) Virginia Tech 90-91

Jones, Joe (DE) Tennessee State 70-71, 73, 75-78

Jones, Keith (RB) Nebraska 89

Jones, Kirk (RB) UNLV *87

Jones, Marlon (DE) Central State 87-89

Jones, Reginald (CB) Memphis State #94

Jones, Ricky (LB) Tuskegee 77-79

Jones, Ricky (WR) Alabama State ##92

Jones, Selwyn (DB) Colorado State 93-#94

Jones, Tony (OT) Western Carolina 88-95

Jordan, Henry (DT) Virginia 57-58

Jordan, Homer (QB) Clemson *87

Junkin, Mike (LB) Duke 87-88

K

Kafentzis, Mark (S) Hawaii 82

Kanicki, Jim (DT) Michigan State 63-69

Kapter, Alex (G) Northwestern 46-47

Katolin, Mike (C) San Jose State *87

Kauric, Jerry (K) Kennedy Collegiate 90

Kellermann, Ernie (DB) Miami (Ohio) 66-71

Kelley, Chris (TE) Akron *87

Kelly, Leroy (RB) Morgan State 64-73
Kemp, Perry (WR) California (Pa.) *87
Killian, P.J. (LB) Virginia ##94
Kinard, Billy (DB) Mississippi 56
Kinchen, Brian (TE) Louisiana State 91-95
King, Don (T) Kentucky 54
King, Ed (OL) Auburn 91-93
King, Joe (DB) Oklahoma State 91
Kingrea, Rick (LB) Tulane 71-72
Kirk, Randy (LB) San Diego State 91
Kissell, John (T) Boston College 50-52, 54-56
Kmet, Frank (NT) Purdue ##92
Kolesar, Bob (G) Michigan 46
Konz, Ken (DB) Louisiana State 53-59
Kosar, Bernie (QB) Miami (Fla.) 85-93
Kosikowski, Frank (WR) Notre Dame 48
Kovaleski, Mike (LB) Notre Dame *87
Kramer, Kyle (S) Bowling Green 89
Kreitling, Rich (WR) Illinois 59-63
Krerowicz, Mark (G) Ohio State #85
Kuechenberg, Rudy (LB) Purdue *87

L

Lahr, Warren (DB) Western Reserve 48-59
Landry, George (RB) Lamar *87
Lane, Gary (QB) Missouri 66-67
Langham, Antonio (CB) Alabama 94-95
Langhorne, Reggie (WR) Elizabeth City State 85-91
Lauter, Steve (S) San Diego State *87
Lavelli, Dante (WR) Ohio State 46-56
Lee, Barry (C) Grambling *87
Lee, Marcus (RB) Syracuse 94
Lefear, Billy (WR) Henderson State 72-75
Leigh, Charles (RB) No College 68-69
Leomiti, Carlson (OL) San Diego State ##94
LeVeck, Jack (LB) Ohio 75
Lewis, Cliff (QB) Duke 46-51
Lewis, Darryl (TE) Texas-Arlington 84
Lewis, Leo (PR) Missouri 90
Lewis, Stan (DE) Wayne (Neb.) 75
Lilja, George (G-T) Michigan 84-86
Linden, Errol (T) Houston 61
Lindsey, Dale (LB) Western Kentucky 65-72
Lingenfeiter, Bob (T) Nebraska 77
Lingmerth, Goran (K) Northern Arizona *87
Lloyd, Dave (LB) Georgia 59-61
Logan, Dave (WR) Colorado 76-83
Logan, Ernie (DL) East Carolina 91-93
London, Tom (DB) North Carolina State 78
Long, Mel (LB) Toledo 72-74
Loomis, Ace (RB) LaCrosse State 52
Lucci, Mike (LB) Tennessee 62-64

Luck, Terry (QB) Nebraska 77
Luneberg, Chris (OL) West Chester ##93
Lund, Bill (RB) Case Tech 46-47
Lyle, Rick (DE) Missouri 94, #95
Lyons, Damion (DB) UCLA ##94
Lyons, Robert (S) Akron 89

M

Maceau, Mel (C) Marquette 46-48
Macerelli, John (G) St. Vincent 56
Mack, Kevin (RB) Clemson 85-93
Majors, Bobby (DB) Tennessee 72
Malone, Ralph (DE) Georgia Tech 86
Manoa, Tim (FB) Penn State 87-89
Marangi, Gary (QB) Boston College #77
Marshall, Dave (LB) Eastern Michigan 84
Marshall, Jim (DE) Ohio State 60
Martin,Jim (DT) Notre Dame 50
Mason,Larry (RB) Troy State *87
Massey, Carlton (DE) Texas 54-56
Matheson, Bob (LB) Duke 67-70
Matthews, Clay (LB) Southern California 78-93
Mayne, Lewis (RB) Texas 47
Mays, Dave (QB) Texas Southern 76-77
McCade, Mike (WR) Nevada–Las Vegas *87
McCardell, Keenan (WR) Nevada–Las Vegas 92-95
McClung, Willie (DT) Florida A&M 58-59
McCollum, Andy (OL) Toledo ##94
McCormack, Mike (T) Kansas 54-62
McCusker, Jim (DE) Ohio State 63
McDonald, Paul (QB) Southern California 80-85
McDonald, Tommy (WR) Oklahoma 68
McGonnigal, Bruce (TE) Virginia 91
McKay, Bob (T) Texas 70-75
McKenzie, Rich (DE) Penn State 95
McKinnis, Hugh (RB) Arizona State 73-75
McLemore, Tom (TE) Southern 93-94
McMahon, Jim (QB) Brigham Young #95
McMillan, Erik (S) Missouri 93
McNeil, Clifton (WR) Grambling 64-67
McNeil, Gerald (WR/KR) Baylor 86-89
Memmelaar, Dale (G) Wyoming 64-65
Metcalf,Eric (RB) Texas 89-94
Meylan, Wayne (LB) Nebraska 68-69
Michaels, Walter (LB) Washington & Lee 52-61
Middleton, Ron (TE) Auburn 89
Miller, Cleo (RB) Arkansas AM&N 75-82
Miller, Mark (QB) Bowling Green 78-79
Miller, Matt (T) Colorado 79-82
Miller, Nick (LB) Arkansas 87
Miller, Willie (WR) Colorado State 75-76
Milstead, Rod (G) Delaware State #93
Minniear, Randy (RB) Purdue 70

Minnifield, Frank (CB) Louisville 84-92
Mitchell, Alvin (DB) Morgan State 68-69
Mitchell, Bobby (RB) Illinois 58-61
Mitchell, Mack (DE) Houston 75-78
Modzelewski, Dick (DT) Maryland 64-66
Modzelewski, Ed (RB) Maryland 55-59
Mohring, John (LB) C.W. Post 80
Montgomery, Cleotha (KR) Abiline Christian 81
Moog, Aaron (DE) Nevada–Las Vegas *87
Moore, Eric (OL) Indiana 95
Moore, Stevon (DB) Mississippi 92-95
Moriarty, Pat (RB) Georgia Tech 79
Morin, Milt (TE) Massachusetts 66-75
Morris, Chris (T) Indiana 72-73
Morris, Joe (RB) Syracuse 91
Morris, Mike (C) Northeast Mississippi State 90
Morrison, Fred (RB) Ohio State 54-56
Morrison, Reece (RB) Southwest Texas State 68-72
Morrow, John (C) Michigan 60-66
Morze, Frank (C) Boston College 62-63
Moseley, Mark (K) Stephen F. Austin 86
Mosselle, Dom (RB) Superior (Wisconsin) State College 50
Mostardi, Richard (DB) Kent State 60
Motley, Marion (RB) Nevada 46-53
Murphy, Fred (WR) Georgia Tech. 60
Mustafaa, Najee (CB) Georgia Tech 93
Myslinski, Tom (OL) Tennessee ##92

N

Nagler, Gern (WR) Santa Clara 60-61
Nave,Stevan (LB) Kansas *87
Nelsen, Bill (QB) Southern California 68-72
Neujahr, Quentin (OL) Kansas State #95
Newman, Patrick (WR) San Diego State 94
Newsome, Ozzie (TE) Alabama 78-90
Newsome, Vince (DB) Washington 91-92
Nicolas, Scott (LB) Miami 82-86
Ninowski, Jim (QB) Michigan State 58-59, 62-66
Noll, Chuck (G-LB) Dayton 53-59
Nugent, Terry (QB) Colorado State #84
Nutting, Ed (DT) Georgia Tech. 61

O

O'Brien, Francis (T) Michigan State 59
O'Connell, Tom (QB) Illinois 56-57
O'Connor, Bill (DE) Notre Dame 49
Oden, McDonald (TE) Tennessee State 80-82
Odom, Clifton (LB) Texas-Arlington 80
Oliphant, Mike (RB) Puget Sound 89-91
Oliver, Bob (DE) Abilene Christian 69
Oristaglio, Bob (DE) Pennsylvania 51

Owens, Kerry (LB) Arkansas ##89

P

Pagel, Mike (QB) Arizona State 86-90

Palelei, Lonnie (OL) Nevada–Las Vegas #95

Palmer, Darrell (DT) Texas Christian 49-53

Palumbo, Sam (LB) Notre Dame 55-56

Parilli, Vito (QB) Kentucky 56

Parker, Frank (DT) Oklahoma State 62-64, 66-67

Parker, Jerry (LB) Central State *87

Parris, Gary (TE) Florida State 75-78

Parrish, Bernie (DB) Florida 59-66

Parseghian, Ara (RB) Miami (Ohio) 48-49

Patten, Joel (T) Duke 80

Paul, Don (DB) Washington State 54-58

Payton, Eddie (KR) Jackson State 77

Peebles, Danny (WR) North Carolina State 91

Pena, Bob (G) Massachusetts 72

Perini, Pete (RB) Ohio State 55

Perry, Michael Dean (DE) Clemson 88-94

Perry, Rod (CB) Colorado 83-84

Peters, Floyd (DT) San Francisco State 59-62

Peters, Tony (DB) Oklahoma 75-78

Petersen, Ted (T) Eastern Illinois 84

Petitbon, John (DB) Notre Dame 55-56

Phelps, Don (RB) Kentucky 50-51

Philcox, Todd (QB) Syracuse 91-93

Phipps, Mike (QB) Purdue 70-76

Pierce, Calvin (FB) Eastern Illinois *87

Pierce, Steve (WR) Illinois *87

Pietrosante, Nick (RB) Notre Dame 66-67

Pike, Chris (DL) Tulsa 89-90

Piskor, Ray (T) Niagara 47

Pitts, Frank (WR) Southern 71-73

Pitts, John (DB) Arizona State 75

Pizzo, Joe (QB) Mars Hill *87

Pleasant, Anthony (DE) Tennessee State 90-95

Plum, Milt (QB) Penn State 57-61

Polley, Tom (LB) Nevada–Las Vegas *87

Poole, Larry (RB) Kent State 75-77

Poumele, Pulu (G) Arizona ##95

Powell, Craig (LB) Ohio State 95

Powell, Preston (RB) Grambling 61

Powers, Ricky (RB) Michigan 95

Prestel, Jim (T) Idaho 60

Pritchett, Billy (RB) West Texas State 75

Pruitt, Greg (RB) Oklahoma 73-81

Pruitt, Mike (RB) Purdue 76-84

Ptacek, Bob (QB) Michigan 59

Pucci, Ben (DT) No College 48

Putnam, Duane (G) College of Pacific 61

Pupua, Tau (DT) Weber State #95

Puzzuoli, Dave (NT) Pittsburgh 83-87

Q

Quinlan, Bill (DE) Michigan State 57-58

Quinlan, Voiney (RB) San Diego State 56

Quinton, Dustin (OL) Nevada–Las Vegas ##91

R

Raimey, Dave (DB) Michigan 64

Rakoczy, Gregg (OL) Miami 87-90

Ratterman, George (QB) Notre Dame 52-56

Rechichar, Bert (DB) Tennessee 52

Redden, Barry (RB) Richmond 89-90

Reeves, Ken (OL) Texas A&M 90

Reeves, Walter (TE) Auburn 94-95

Renfro, Ray (WR) North Texas St. 52-63

Reynolds, Billy (RB) Pittsburgh 53-54, 57

Reynolds, Chuck (C) Tulsa 69-70

Rhome, Jerry (QB) Tulsa 69

Rich, Randy (DB) New Mexico 78-79

Richardson, Gloster (WR) Jackson State 72-74

Riddick, Louis (DB) Pittsburgh 93-95

Rienstra, John (OL) Temple 91-92

Righetti, Joe (DT) Waynesburg 69-70

Risien, Cody (T) Texas A&M 79-83, 85-89

Rison, Andre (WR) Michigan State 95

Roan, Oscar (TE) Southern Methodist 75-78

Robbins, Kevin (OT) Michigan State ##89, 90

Roberts, Walter (WR) San Jose State 64-66

Robinson, Billy (DB) Arizona State *87

Robinson, DeJuan (DB) Northern Arizona *87

Robinson, Fred (G) Washington 57

Robinson, Mike (DE) Arizona 81-82

Rockins, Chris (S) Oklahoma State 84-87

Rogers, Don (S) UCLA 84-85

Rokisky, John (DE) Duquesne 46

Roman, Nick (DE) Ohio State 72-74

Romaniszyn, Jim (LB) Edinboro State 73-74

Rose, Ken (LB) Nevada–Las Vegas 90

Rouson, Lee (RB) Colorado 91

Rowe, Patrick (WR) San Diego State 93

Rowell, Eugene (WR) Southern Mississippi 90

Rucker, Reggie (WR) Boston University 75-81

Runager, Max (P) South Carolina 88

Rusinek, Mike (NT) California *87

Ryan, Frank (QB) Rice 62-68

Rymkus, Lou (T) Notre Dame 46-51

Rypien, Mark (QB) Washington State 94

S

Saban, Lou (LB) Indiana 46-49

Sabatino, Bill (DT) Colorado 68

Sagapolutele, Pio (DL) Hawaii 91-95

St. Clair, Mike (DE) Grambling 76-79

Sandusky, John (T) Villanova 50-55

Sanford, Lucius (LB) Georgia Tech 87

Scales, Charley (RB) Indiana 62-65

Scarry, Mike (C) Waynesburg 46-47

Schafrath, Dick (G-T) Ohio State 59-71

Schoen, Tom (DB) Notre Dame 70

Schultz, Randy (RB) State College (Iowa) 66

Schwenk, Bud (QB) Washington 46

Scott, Bo (RB) Ohio State 69-74

Scott, Clarence (DB) Kansas State 71-83

Sczurek, Stan (LB) Purdue 63-65

Seifert, Mike (DE) Wisconsin 74

Selawski, Gene (T) Purdue 60

Sensanbaugher, Dean (RB) Ohio State 48

Sharkey, Ed (G) Nevada 53

Shavers, Tyrone (WR) Lamar 91

Sheppard, Henry (G-T) Southern Methodist 76-81

Sheriff, Stan (G) California Poly 57

Sherk, Jerry (DT) Oklahoma State 70-81

Shiner, Dick (QB) Maryland 67

Shoals, Roger (T) Maryland 63-64

Shofner, Jim (DB) Texas Christian 58-63

Shorter, Jim (DB) Detroit 62-63

Shula, Don (DB) John Carroll 51-52

Shurnas, Marshall (WR) Missouri 47

Sikich, Mike (G) Northwestern 71

Sikora, Robert (T) Indiana #84

Simonetti, Len (DT) Tennessee 46-48

Simons, Kevin (OT) Tennessee ##89

Sims, Darryl (DE) Wisconsin *87-88

Sims, Mickey (DT) South Carolina State 77-79

Sipe, Brian (QB) San Diego State 74-83

Skibinski, Joe (G) Purdue 52

Slaughter, Webster (WR) San Diego State 86-91

Slayden, Steve (QB) Duke #88

Smith, Bob (LB) Nebraska 55-56

Smith, Daryle (OT) Tennessee 89

Smith, Gaylon (RB) Southwestern 46

Smith, Jim Ray (G) Baylor 56-62

Smith, John (WR) Tennessee State 79

Smith, Ken (TE) New Mexico 73

Smith, Leroy (LB) Iowa ##92

Smith, Ralph (TE) Mississippi 65-68

Smith, Rico (WR) Colorado 92-95

Snidow, Ron (DE) Oregon 68-72

Sparenberg, Dave (G) Western Ontario *87

Speedie, Mac (WR) Utah 46-52

Speer, Del (S) Florida 93-94

Spencer, Joe (DT) Oklahoma State 49

Stams, Frank (LB) Notre Dame 92-95

Stanfield, Harold (TE) West Virginia Tech *87

Staroba, Paul (WR) Michigan 72

Steinbrunner, Don (DE) Washington State 53

Stephens, Larry (DT) Texas 60-61

Steuber, Bob (RB) Missouri 46

Stevenson, Rickey (CB) Arizona 70

Stewart, Andrew (DE) Cincinnati 89

Stienke, Jim (DB) Southwest Texas State 73

Stover, Matt (K) Louisiana State 91-95

Stracka, Tim (TE) Wisconsin 83-84

Strock, Don (QB) Virginia Tech 88

Sullivan, Dave (WR) Virginia 73-74

Sullivan, Gerry (T-C) Illinois 74-81

Sullivan,Tom (RB) Miami (Fla.) 78

Summers, Fred (DB) Wake Forest 69-71

Sumner, Walt (DB) Florida State 69-74

Sustersic, Ed (RB) Findlay 49

Sutter, Ed (LB) Northwestern ##92, 93-95

Swarn, George (RB) Miami (Ohio) *87

Swilling, Ken (LB) Georgia Tech ##92

T

Taffoni, Joe (T) Tennessee-Martin 67-70

Talley, John (TE) West Virginia ##89-91

Tamm, Ralph (G) West Chester State 90-91

Taseff, Carl (DB) John Carroll 51

Taylor, Terry (CB) Southern Illinois 92-93

Teets, Dick (LB) Wisconsin *87

Teifke, Mike (C) Akron *87

Tennell, Derek (TE) UCLA *87-89

Terlep, George (QB) Notre Dame 48

Terrell, Ray (RB) Mississippi 46-47

Testaverde, Vinny (QB) Miami (Fla.) 93-95

Thaxton, Jim (TE) Tennessee State 74

Thomas, Johnny (CB) Baylor 95

Thome, Chris (OL) Minnesota 91-92

Thompson, Bennie (DB) Grambling 94-95

Thompson, T. (C) William & Mary 49-53

Thornton, John (DL) Cincinnati 91

Tidmore, Sam (LB) Ohio State 62-63

Tierney, Leo (C) Georgia Tech. 78

Tillman, Lawyer (WR) Auburn 89, 92-93

Tinsley, Keith (WR) Pittsburgh *87

Tomczak, Mike (QB) Ohio State 92

Trocano, Rick (DB-QB) Pittsburgh 81-83

Trumbull, Rick (OL) Missouri ##91

Tucker, Travis (TE) Southern Connecticut State 85-87

Tupa, Tom (QB-P) Ohio State #93, 94-95

Turnbow, Jese (DT) Tennessee 78

Turner, Eric (S) UCLA 91-95

Turner, Kevin (LB) Pacific 82

U

Ulinski, Ed (G) Marshall 46-49

Upshaw, Marvin (DE) Trinity 68-69

V

Van Dyke, Ralph (T) Southern Illinois *87

Van Pelt, Brad (LB) Michigan State 86

Vardell, Tommy (RB) Stanford 92-95

Verser, David (WR) Kansas *87

W

Wagner, Bryan (P) Cal-State Northridge 89-90

Waiters, Van (LB) Indiana 88-91

Walker, Dwight (RB-WR) Nicholls State 82-84

Wallace, Calvin (DE) West Virginia Tech *87

Walls, Everson (DB) Grambling 92-93

Walters, Dale (P) Rice *87

Ward, Carl (DB) Michigan 67-68

Warfield, Paul (WR) Ohio State 64-69, 76-77

Washington, Brian (S) Nebraska 88

Watkins, Tom (RB) Iowa State 61

Watson, Karlton (QB) Winston-Salem *87

Watson, Louis (WR) Miss. Val. St. *87

Watson, Remi (WR) Bethune-Cookman *87

Weathers, Clarence (WR) Delaware State 85-88

Weathers, Curtis (TE-LB) Mississippi 79-85

Webb, Ken (RB) Presbyterian 63

Weber, Chuck (DE) West Chester State 55-56

Webster, Larry (DT) Maryland 95

White, Bob (RB) Stanford 55

White, Charles (RB) Southern California 80-82, 84

White, James (DE) Louisiana State #85

White, Lorenzo (RB) Michigan State 95

Whitlow, Bob (C) Arizona 68

Whitwell, Mike (WR-S) Texas A&M 82-83

Wiggin, Paul (DE) Stanford 57-67

Wilburn, Barry (CB) Mississippi 92

Wilkerson, Gary (DB) Penn State ##89

Wilkinson, Jerry (DE) Oregon State 80

Williams, A.D. (WR) College of Pacific 60

Williams, Arthur (WR) Abilene Christian *87

Williams, Clarence(H-B) Washington State 93

Williams, Gene (T-G) Iowa State 93-94

Williams, Larry (G) Notre Dame 86-88

Williams, Lawrence (KR) Texas Tech 77

Williams, Ray (WR) Clemson *87

Williams, Sidney (LB) Southern 64-66

Williams, Stacy (DB) East Texas State *87

Williams, Tony (T) Kansas State 93

Williams, Wally (C) Florida A&M 93-95

Willis, Bill (G-LB) Ohio State 46-53

Wilson, Tom (RB) No College 62

Wilson, Troy (CB) Notre Dame *87

Wingle, Blake (G) UCLA *87

Winslow, George (P) Villanova 87

Winters, Frank (C) Western Illinois 87-88

Wise, Mike (DL) California–Davis 91

Wiska, Jeff (G) Michigan State 86

Wolfley, Ron (RB) West Virginia 92-93

Woods, Rob (OL) Arizona 91

Woolsey, Rolly (DB) Boise State 77

Wooten, John (G) Colorado 59-67

Wren, Junior (DB) Missouri 56-59

Wright, Alvin (NT) Jacksonville State 92

Wright, Felix (S) Drake 85-90

Wright, George (DT) Sam Houston 72

Wright, Keith (WR-KR) Memphis State 78-80

Wycinsky, Craig (G) Michigan State 72

Y

Yanchar, Bill (DT) Purdue 70

Yonaker, John (DE) Notre Dame 46-49

Young, George (DE) Georgia 46-53

Young, Glen (WR) Mississippi 84-85, 87-88

Youngblood, George (DB) California State (Los Angeles) 67

Youngelman, Sid (DT) Alabama 59

Z

Zeir, Eric (QB) Georgia 95

Zeno, Lance (C) UCLA 92-93

Roster includes players, 1946-95

* Denotes replacement player during 1987 players' strike.

On active roster, but did not play in a game.

On practice squad, but did not play in a game.

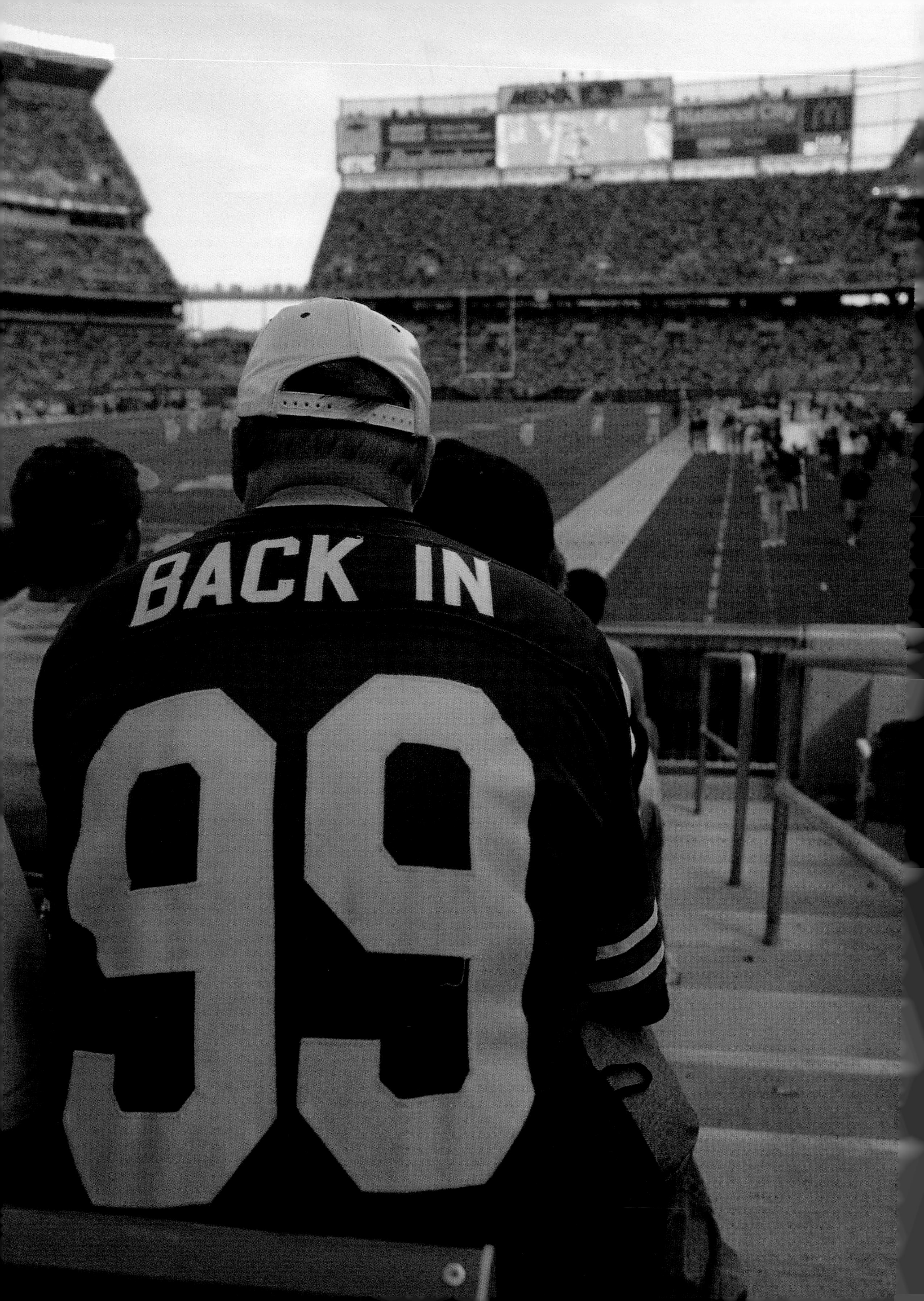
BACK IN
99

BACK HOME

BACK HOME

VOLUME II

The Birth of Cleveland Browns Stadium

Editor

Tim Graham

Design

Tom Morgan

Associate Editor

Rich Exner

Senior Writer

Dan Coughlin

Contributing Writers

Steve Herrick

Fred Greetham

Senior Photographer

Ron Kuntz

Contributing Photographers

Janine Exner

Roger Mastroianni

Stephen S. Counsel

Elizabeth Fulford Schiau

John H. Reid III

WOODFORD PRESS

Printed in Canada.

Book and cover design: Tom Morgan, Blue
Design, www.bluedes.com

Library of Congress Catalog Card Number
available upon request.
ISBN: 0-942627-69-5

Distributed by Andrews McMeel Publishing,
Kansas City, MO.

Woodford Press
5900 Hollis Street, Suite K
Emeryville, CA 94608

C. David Burgin, Editor and Publisher
Daniel C. Ross, CEO and Publisher
William F. Duane, Senior Vice President

Associate Publishers:
Franklin M. Dumm
William W. Scott, Esq.
William B. McGuire, Esq.

PAGE 2: Workers install the sound system
during final stages of construction in June
1999. The 435,000-watt system employs 640
speakers in the seating areas.

RIGHT: Part of the crowd of 73,138 at Opening
Night of the regular season, September 12,
1999.

PAGES 6 AND 7: Darrin Chiaverini's block of
New England's Chris Carter opened the door
for Kevin Johnson to become the first Brown
to score a touchdown in Cleveland Browns
Stadium during the regular season. The
touchdown came during the first quarter of
the second home game, October 3, 1999.

Contents

"We're talking about something that is more than a stadium, more than a baseball team, more than a basketball team. It's what this city wants to become in the 21st century."

—GOV. RICHARD F. CELESTE, VOICING HIS SUPPORT FOR THE 1990 SIN TAX CAMPAIGN TO BUILD JACOBS FIELD AND GUND ARENA.

1. CLEVELAND'S NEW JEWEL

The Grandest Opening

BY TIM GRAHAM

PAGE 10: Mayor Michael White, whose leadership helped ensure the Browns would be reborn in Cleveland, during groundbreaking ceremonies for Cleveland Browns Stadium in May 1997.

PAGES 10 AND 11: Cleveland Browns Stadium — shown here moments before the kickoff in the first game, a preseason meeting with the Minnesota Vikings on August 12, 1999 — represents the latest in a string of civic successes for Cleveland.

LEFT: Work begins on the framework for the giant scoreboards in June 1999.

The day dawned as so many summer mornings do in northern Ohio, under clear skies with only a trace of white clouds on the distant horizon, a sign that it would probably cloud over before noon.

On this day the skies turned gray even earlier, and when the Minnesota Vikings joined hands in the courtyard of the Airport Marriott for meditation and prayer early that afternoon, the prospect of thunderstorms threatened to do more than any opposing team possibly could to spoil the day for Cleveland. ➤

This was a moment Cleveland had awaited for three years and eight months. It had been 1,343 days since the last Cleveland Browns home game. Where that game had been played in a decaying stadium before broken hearts mourning the past, this was a day to cheer the promise of greater glory to come. It was a day to celebrate the opening of a spectacular new stadium on the same spot where yesterday's heroes won the hearts of Browns' fans forever.

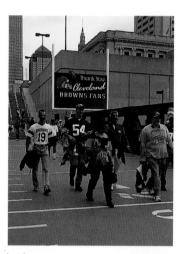

Fans began crossing the bridge from downtown to the new stadium hours before the gates opened for the first preseason game.

It didn't matter that this was just a preseason game, and it wouldn't count for anything officially. What mattered was that 1,343 was being pushed back to 0.

Hundreds of fans began lining up outside the stadium well before the gates opened two hours before the kickoff. They came from all over Ohio and from many distant states. Standing among them, on the concourse overlooking Lake Erie, was the legendary Lou Groza, looking good just a few months shy of his famous number 76.

One of the first sensations to hit the fans was how much closer they felt to the action. Bruce and Sharon Weaver, new season-ticket holders from Sandusky, were thrilled with the view from their seats in the lower deck, above the end zone in the northeast corner of the stadium. "We're so close to the field," said Sharon Weaver. "In the old stadium you were so far away, it was better to stay home and watch on TV."

Retired Cleveland steelworker Tim Smith, a Browns fan for more than 40 years, was pleased with his seats in the new Dawg Pound. "Especially this bench," he said, pounding on the seat backs that were added to the bleachers.

So what was it like from the highest perch in the upper deck? Cincinnati schoolteacher Chris Gutermuth, from his seat in Section 543, Row 32, Seat 15, in the northwest corner of the stadium, could see the sun setting behind him and watch sailboats gracing the lake to his left. Scanning from left to right he enjoyed a fabulous view of planes landing at Burke Lakefront Airport. In front of him was the scoreboard

A thunderous ovation
greeted the Browns as
they ran onto the field
through an inflatable
helmet before the game
against the Vikings.

and its giant TV screen, flanked by the American flag on one side and the Marine Corps flag on the other, and to his right was the downtown skyline. He seemed to be right on top of the field, even though he was the equivalent of 12 stories above it. "It's a beautiful view," he said.

And the best part, said Frank Reese, with his family just a few seats away, "There's no pole obstructing your view."

About an hour before the game, as if on cue, the clouds started to break up. The brilliant green turf and orange seats were bathed in sunshine. Soon familiar chants came forth. "Here we go, Brownies, here we go. Woof! Woof! Here we go, Brownies, here we go!"

"It's like a playoff game," Dave Sutherland, a season ticket holder since 1987 from Erie, Pa., said of the atmosphere before kickoff.

At 7:06 p.m., on August 21, 1999, with at least seven airplanes and helicopters, plus the Goodyear blimp, circling the stadium, Minnesota kicker Mitch Berger placed the ball on the tee. As he booted the ball 61 yards toward the Dawg Pound, the stadium sparkled with the lights of flash cameras in a scene evocative of an Olympics opening ceremony. Ronnie Powell caught the ball on the 9 and made an unforgettable dash to the 31, where Corey Miller brought him down. Never have fans cheered louder for a 22-yard return.

James Juliano, from Bloomfield Hills, Mich., arrived with his wife just in time for the kickoff. Never before had he come to a Browns game, but he didn't want to miss the moment. "We're football fans," he said as he waited for an usher to find his seat, "and this is something historic."

As the cheers subsided, Juliano turned and exclaimed, "What a beautiful stadium!"

More than three hours later, the game ended with the Browns on the short end of a 24-17 score. In the closing seconds, the Browns still had a chance to win. But a Vikings interception in the end zone, on a play reminiscent of one at the opposite end of the field that spoiled the Browns' drive to the Super Bowl in 1981, ended the comeback bid.

On this night, though, there was no sadness. Only tears of joy.

PAGES 16 AND 17: In the first of what promised to be a long string of sellouts, 71,398 fans attended the first game in Cleveland Browns Stadium on August 21, 1999.

PAGES 18 AND 19: Minnesota kicked to Cleveland to start the game.

Even practice was exciting

BY RICH EXNER

How much did Clevelanders miss their Browns?

An estimated 100,000 people toured the new stadium the weekend before the first preseason game, and many more were turned away. Some of the lucky ones waited more than two hours before getting inside for a quick peek.

About 20,000 season-ticket holders and other invited guests turned out for the team's first practice in the new digs, and it was a Tuesday afternoon.

Police estimated the crowd at 50,000 for a downtown parade and rally on the afternoon before the first game.

And remember, all this was the buildup for the first of two preseason home games. There was no point trying to tell football-starved Browns fans that these games didn't count.

Their Brownies were back, and anyone just passing through town could not have missed it.

The hottest new clothing fashion had become brown football jerseys with 2s and 54s on them. Orange was the paint color of choice, whether it was being put to use on an old bus in an effort to make the game transportation look like a football helmet, or on yard signs in most every suburb.

LEFT: Terry Kirby and Mark Edwards during practice.

ABOVE RIGHT: Mike Kelley of Grafton, Ohio, watches the Browns train in Berea from the roof of his car in a nearby parking lot.

The atmosphere was reminiscent of the Browns' last glory days of playoff football in the mid-1980s, when the statues standing guard in front of the Federal Reserve Bank wore Browns helmets, and street salesmen hawking Browns souvenirs outnumbered lunchtime hot-dog vendors.

Only this time, winning was not as important.

At this point in the new Browns' history, it wasn't whether they won or lost, but that they played the game.

PAGES 24 AND 25: The barking begins on the first day of training camp as rookies Ryan Taylor, Kendall Ogle and Arnold Miller step onto the practice field for the first time.

LEFT: Kendall Ogle autographs the hard hat of fan Migdalla Gonzalez of Elyria.

RIGHT: For more than two years, a clock in Tower City counted down the days until the Browns would return to Cleveland for their first preseason game, on August 21, 1999.

Cleveland Browns Stadium, by the numbers

- **$283** million cost, financed with funding from the city of Cleveland, Cuyahoga County, state of Ohio, Regional Transit Authority, the Cleveland Browns and a loan from Cleveland Tomorrow.

- **73,200** seats, including **8,600** club seats, **2,700** suite seats, **10,000** Dawg Pound bench seats and **700** wheelchair seats.

- **One** traditional name, Cleveland Browns Stadium, a rarity in an era of stadiums named for corporate sponsors.

- **Four** gates, each named for a different corporate sponsor in an arrangement that made it possible for the stadium to be named for the Browns. There's the STERIS Gate in the Northeast corner, the CoreComm Gate in the Northwest corner, Cleveland Clinic Sports Health Gate in the Southwest corner and National City Gate in the Southeast corner.

- **147** luxury suites, each with maple woodwork and black accents matching the décor in the Browns' locker room. Each suite has a private restroom, closet, a refrigerator (some have two), four televisions and outdoor seating areas equipped with special radiant-heating systems under the chairs.

- **12** ticket windows, nine passenger elevators, four escalators and two freight elevators.

- **Two** giant scoreboards, the largest in any NFL stadium, above each end zone. Each video board is **27** feet tall and **94** feet wide, encompassing **2,228** square feet. A crew of **25** operates the scoreboards and **450,000**-watt sound system with **640** speakers.

- **70** restrooms, **41** women's and **29** men's. **948** toilets (more than three times as many as in Municipal Stadium), **391** urinals, **204** sinks and **51** drinking fountains.

- **Four** locker rooms. The Browns' is **11,000** square feet, with solid maple lockers and deep carpets. It will be used exclusively by the Browns. When the stadium hosts other events, the two visitors' locker rooms, each with **5,000** square feet, will be used. The fourth locker room, with **1,600** square feet, is for officials.

- **592** stadium lights, each with **1,500**-watt fixtures (**528** are conventional metal halide, and **64** are double-ended hot-restart fixtures).

- **24,703** trees, plants and flowers.

- **43** permanent and **61** portable concession stands.

- **63,200** cup holders, one for every seat except those in the Dawg Pound.

- **31** acres, or **1.64** million square feet, comprise the stadium site. The highest point is equal to a **12**-story building.

The playing field has
Kentucky bluegrass turf.
It is irrigated and has a
sand base. The field has
an underground heating
system containing nine
boilers and 40 miles of
underground piping. The
heating system is
designed to prevent the

LEFT AND ABOVE: Young fans can dream of touchdowns even before reaching their seats in Cleveland Browns Stadium. This new commuter station opened just in time for the stadium's opening. It's the sixth stop on Cleveland's Waterfront train line. The Greater Cleveland Regional Transit Authority spent $70 million to build the Waterfront line in 1996. From the Stadium, riders can head to the transit's hub underneath Terminal Tower, then connect to four other lines, including one to Cleveland Hopkins International Airport.

PAGES 34-35: A crew of 25 skilled professionals operates the giant scoreboards from a control center adjacent to the press box.

RIGHT AND ABOVE:
Cleveland Browns
Stadium has 148 luxury
suites, each with maple
woodwork and black
accents matching those
in the Browns' locker
room. Each suite has a
private restroom, closet,
refrigerator, four
televisions and outdoor
seating areas equipped
with special radiant
heating systems under
the chairs.

- **5,300** tons of reinforced steel, **600** truckloads of concrete weighing **235** million pounds, and **771,463** square feet of masonry walls. More than **14,500** square feet of granite surround the base.

- **469** miles of cable for telecommunications, security, broadcast and audio systems, and **11.65** miles of plumbing pipes.

- **Six** broadcast booths, a national television booth and a **3,696**-square-foot area for working members of the news media in the press box, located on the South side of the stadium.

How the Pound got its bark

BY DAN COUGHLIN

According to urban myth, the first bark in Browns history was born in the throat of Hanford Dixon, a Pro Bowl cornerback.

Upon further review, however, it appears that the first bark might have been uttered by defensive tackle Dave Puzzuoli.

On the other hand, the inaugural snarl could be attributed to linebacker Eddie Johnson.

Momentous events in world history are like that. They are usually evolutionary and sometimes accidental. Columbus, for example, set sail for the East Indies and discovered the Bahamas instead. President John F. Kennedy is credited with inspiring space exploration, but who planted the seed in his mind? It is not the type of thought that would obsess a presidential candidate during a campaign.

So it is with the first bark, which inspired the "Dogs" and later evolved into the phenomenon known as the Dawg Pound, a state of ecstasy officially licensed by the NFL. Not even Columbo could unravel this mystery in a two-hour episode.

One fact everyone seems to accept is that the Dawgs were born in the training camp of 1985 at Lakeland Community College in Mentor.

"We were sitting in a defensive meeting one night watching film," says Johnson, known as "the Assassin" because of his shaved head and

LEFT: John "Big Dawg" Thompson in his house.

The new Dawg Pound is in the same spot as the old one, but it's a kinder, gentler place. The benches have seat backs, but the Dawg Pound is the only seating area that doesn't have cup holders.

fierce demeanor. "We were watching the Pittsburgh Steelers rush the passer and we watched Howie Long of the Raiders maul some poor quarterback. I told Dave Puzzuoli, 'Those guys rush the passer like ferocious dogs.' Dave said, 'Yeah, E.J., if we could get in the game we could make something happen.'

"The defensive players were talking and somebody said that all great defenses have nicknames — the Steel Curtain in Pittsburgh, the Purple People Eaters in Minnesota, the Orange Crush in Denver. Somebody said even the Miami Dolphins and the Killer Bees."

The meeting ended and the subject was dropped. Players went back to their rooms and went to bed.

"But the next morning after breakfast we were walking along a walkway and Puzzuoli barked. I barked back. That's when it started," Johnson contends.

Like the tree falling in the forest, however, no one else heard Johnson and Puzzuoli barking.

Dixon claims responsibility for the first public bark in the same training camp.

"It was at practice," recalls Dixon, then a 26-year-old cornerback in his fifth season with the Browns. "I was trying to get the defensive linemen going, to get a rush on the quarterback. I was thinking the quarterback is the cat and the defensive line is the dogs.

"At Lakeland the fans were close to the practice fields. They heard us barking and they started to bark back. Before you knew it, the whole defense, the whole city was barking. It worked out good. Now you've got people barking all over the United States."

The defensive backs were a particularly close-knit and proud unit. The cornerbacks were Dixon and Frank Minnifield, the safeties were Al Gross and Don Rogers. They were also smart promoters. A year after all

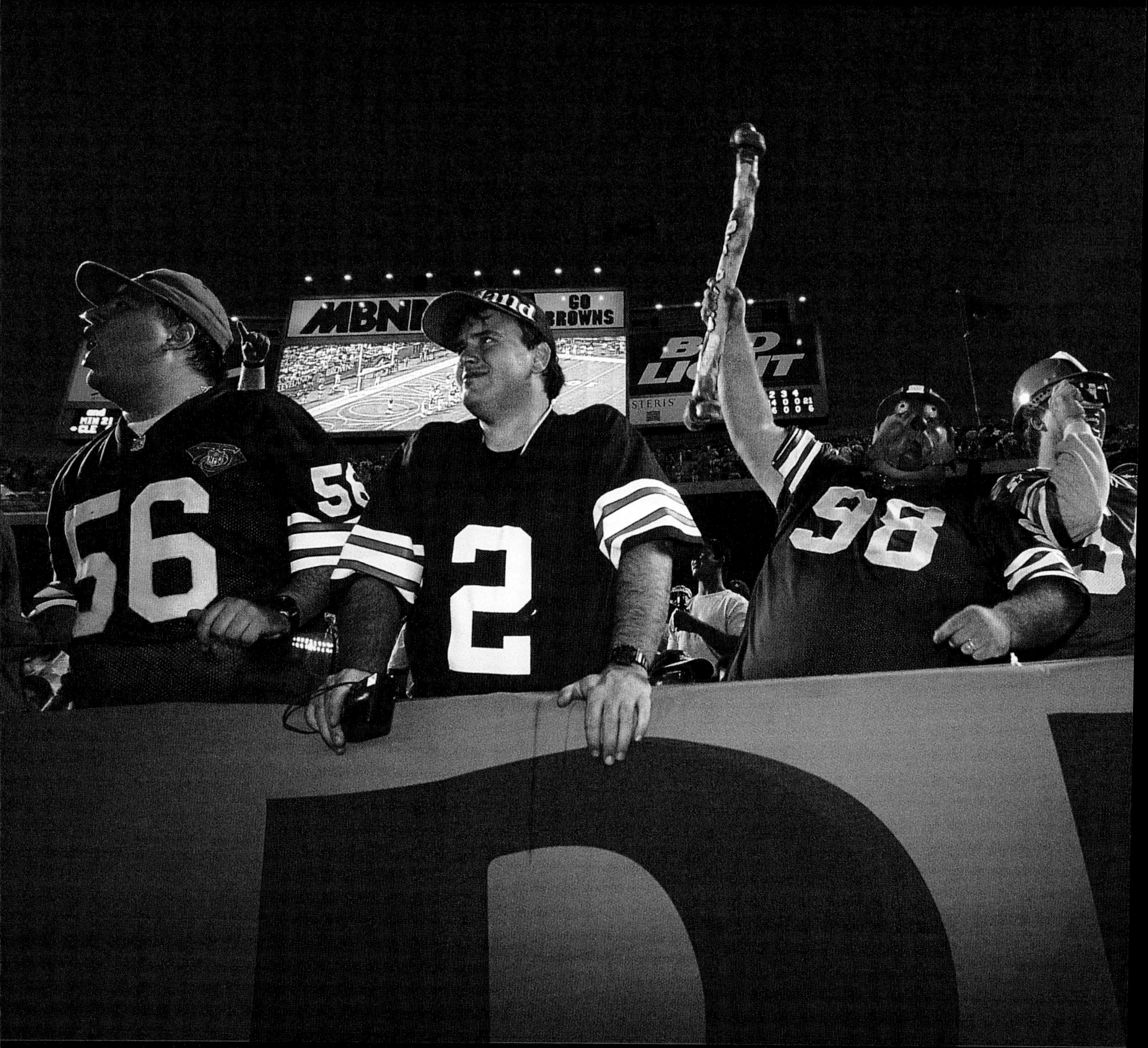
GO
BROWNS
STERIS
56
2
98

this barking began, they realized they were on to something. They seized the moment. The four defensive backs posed on the steps of Cleveland City Hall, each dressed in a white suit and holding a Doberman pinscher by the leash. The poster was titled "Last Line of Defense."

While well-received by the fans, the poster annoyed some on the Browns squad.

"They knew I'd be pissed off," says Johnson.

Nevertheless, the attack-dog persona enveloped the entire team. The Browns attacked in every aspect of the game. Even on offense, the Browns attacked with long passes from Bernie Kosar to Brian Brennan, Reggie Langhorne, Webster Slaughter and Ozzie Newsome. Kevin Mack and Ernest Byner attacked on the ground.

The dog theme even carried over to humorous moments. In describing his role as the nose tackle on the defensive line, Bob Golic said, "I feel like a fireplug at a dog show."

None of this could have been be predicted, of course. It was not part of a grand plan. It was not part of any plan at all.

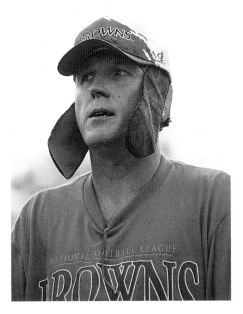

LEFT: The return of the Browns gave the Dawgs plenty to chew on.

RIGHT: Larry Greenshield of Rootstown Township wore Dawg ears to training camp.

The final evolutionary leap involved the fans. The Dawg Pound was not the Dawg Pound yet, but its personality was definitely developing.

The free-standing concrete bleachers of the old Stadium were the cheap seats, separated from the rest of the horseshoe. They accommodated 5,000 fans who sat on unfinished planks with no backs. In stormy weather, the wind blew into their faces, sometimes with hurricane force, toughening them and bonding them into a unique community.

In the 1980s the bleachers became the domain of beer-swilling young fans who seized on the dog persona. They began wearing dog masks and waving bones like weapons. They became magnets for television cameras. One Sunday a fan pelted the visiting team with dog biscuits. The next Sunday 100 fans threw dog biscuits on the field. The fans were unleashed and "the Dawg Pound" entered Cleveland's football vocabulary.

Traditionally, fans have identified with players, but in a weird juxtaposition the Browns players identified with the fans. When the final game of the 1995 season ended, the Browns players ran to the Dawg Pound and embraced the fans in long, tear-filled goodbyes.

Architects kept the Dawg Pound in mind when they designed the

new Cleveland Browns Stadium, although the new ownership made plans to keep the denizens of the Dawg Pound on shorter leashes. Drawing a distinction between enthusiasm and rowdyism, security was increased with zero tolerance for obnoxiousness and vulgarity. The aim was a kinder, gentler Dawg Pound.

In a stunning evolutionary breakthrough, the Dawgs are housebroken.

The Dawgs were unleashed for the first time in their new home on August 21, 1999.

"Teams coming to Ohio are going to understand why the Browns are so special. It's the fans."

—CARMEN POLICY, REACTING TO THE ENTHUSIASM OF THE CROWD
AT THE HALL OF FAME GAME IN CANTON, AUGUST 9, 1999

2. MAKING IT HAPPEN

It began with a Celestial vision
BY RICH EXNER

Any kid who ever played with a shovel and bucket on a sandy beach would understand the concept. Dig a hole close enough to a shoreline with a small channel connecting the two, and water will flow in.

Gov. Richard F. Celeste was the big kid operating the giant hydraulic shovel on July 10, 1986, in the parking lot next to the old Cleveland Stadium. He was joined by a collection of community leaders with grand visions for the future. Cleveland wanted its own version of Baltimore's popular Inner Harbor, hoping to use the Lake Erie waterfront as a catalyst to spark a renaissance in downtown Cleveland. ➤

But since the city didn't have an inner harbor to build around, the state handed over the $8 million needed to create one.

Celeste dug the first chunk of dirt on what was to become a seven-acre expansion of Lake Erie. Those skeptical of such a plan to stimulate growth could have pointed to history.

Even Mayor George V. Voinovich conceded, "Numerous planning studies and development ideas have come forth, but minimal development activity has taken place since the Great Lakes Exposition of 1936 and 1937" at the site.

Voinovich, however, spoke of optimism on that day, saying it would "mark the beginning of our waterfront development." And Celeste predicted the project would be "one of the most significant developments in Cleveland's history."

Although many of the original plans from 1986 have been scrapped (they included replacing the old stadium with a domed one elsewhere downtown to free up lakefront property), all but the most cynical would have to admit that things turned out pretty well.

Literally coming full circle 13 years later, a new Cleveland Browns Stadium opened next door in a much livelier downtown for tourists

LEFT: Cleveland Browns Stadium was designed by HOK Sports Facilities Groups. The construction manager was Huber, Hunt & Nichols.

RIGHT: The construction site as it appeared in September 1997.

and workers alike. Hotels seem to be going up everywhere. There's no shortage of places to find nightlife. And new museums are drawing people who might otherwise never visit downtown Cleveland.

Sports has played a big role in the transformation, in large part because of the creation of 150,000 new seats in four new facilities, while losing only the old Stadium's 80,098 seats.

Cleveland State University got the sports revitalization going in 1991 with the opening of its 13,610-seat Convocation Center, downtown's first new arena since the Cleveland Arena was demolished 14 years earlier.

Then came Jacobs Field (43,368) and Gund Arena (20,562) in 1994, moving the Indians a few blocks to a modern ballpark and the Cavaliers downtown from their rural surroundings of Richfield. And, finally, Cleveland Browns Stadium with 72,300 new orange seats in 1999.

"They are very, very important," Convention & Visitors Bureau spokeswoman Teri Gannon says, "not just with the national recognition with the Browns, Indians and Cavs, but other groups using those facilities as well."

Attractions such as NCAA basketball-tournament games and the U.S. Figure Skating Championships in 2000 are the most obvious bonuses. But Gannon says many groups meeting in Cleveland take advantage of the sports stadiums and arenas when searching for unique meeting or dining venues.

The stadiums are just one factor making Cleveland an easier sell.

"There's definitely more demand than ever. It's been a cumulative effect and the momentum has kept going year after year," Gannon says.

Back when ground was being broken on the inner harbor, Cleveland begged and begged for hotel developers.

It didn't take long to make a round of calls in search of a room. There was Stouffer's Inn on the Square, the Bond Court, the Holiday Inn, the Hollenden and another place or two. Cleveland was a tough sell to attract major conventions because there weren't enough hotel rooms to go around. And hotel developers were reluctant because there wasn't enough guaranteed business.

But by late summer 1999, 11 downtown hotels were open with more than 3,000 rooms for the choosing. Eight more hotels with 1,800 rooms were set to open by spring 2001.

Putting people downtown means creating a lot of business opportunities, many of which are tied together.

Indians owner Richard Jacobs opened his Galleria Shopping Center with 70 stores in 1987, giving the city its first regular nighttime downtown shopping in years.

A second shopping center, the 110-store Avenue at Tower City Center, came on board in 1990, stretching from the heart of downtown — Public Square — cutting underneath the 52-story Terminal Tower and tunneling below two streets before ending with a view of the Cuyahoga River.

"This is only the beginning," Mayor Michael R. White declared at the Avenue's opening ceremony. "We're going to build a new Cleveland, and Tower City Center will be the center."

Since then, the rest of downtown has become a lot more accessible from the center. Tower City was the only downtown stop on the area's commuter train system until the Waterfront Line was added just in time for the city's Bicentennial Celebration in 1996. Trains stop twice in the Flats nightclub district along the Cuyahoga River before heading to the lakefront, with the latest addition being a stop at the football stadium.

And with an indoor walkway from Tower City to the Gund Arena/ Jacobs Field complex, people flying into Cleveland for a basketball game in the dead of winter can leave their coats at home. Just ride the train from the airport to Tower City and then take the short walk to the arena without ever going outside. Even a hotel is connected.

Perhaps the biggest change to downtown Cleveland outside the sports stadiums, however, has been the addition of two museums, which together draw more than 1 million people a year to what is now call North Coast Harbor.

The Great Lakes Science Center opened in 1996 as a solid regional

The Rock and Roll Hall of Fame, dedicated in 1995, as it appears from the Great Lakes Science Center.

draw, and the Rock and Roll Hall of Fame and Museum's dedication in 1995 gave Cleveland an international attraction.

Much like the fight to get the Browns back in town, the quest for the rock hall was a case of civic pride.

Promoters boasted that Cleveland ranked No. 1 in per capita rock record sales, that it was Cleveland disc jockey Alan Freed and record store owner Leo Mintz who coined the phrase "rock 'n' roll" in 1951, and that in 1952 Cleveland hosted the Moon Dog Coronation Ball, described as America's first rock concert.

To drive home the point that Cleveland was a city that cared, petitions with 600,000 signatures of support were handed over to a selection committee considering Cleveland among New York, Los Angeles, St. Louis, Chicago, Boston and other cities.

"It's about winning," Growth Association Vice President Michael Benz said on the eve of the selection committee's visit. "We're not taking anything lightly or disregarding our competition."

But even as the development has circled downtown — from the North Coast Harbor to Playhouse Square, Jacobs Field, the Flats and Cleveland Browns Stadium, plus everything in between — there's a feeling that more work needs to be done.

"You look at the change in the skyline the last 10 years," says Terence J. Uhl, executive director of Cleveland Today, a civic organization that studies and promotes development. "It's a different place and for the better.

"But we need more people living downtown for it to be a more vibrant downtown. There are 3,000 people now. We need to get to 10,000 or 12,000 before it is a 24-hour-a-day downtown."

Promoting downtown residential life and trying to put together plans for a new convention center will be two major initiatives in the coming years. And there's still talk of building an aquarium, which was expected to be an initial cornerstone of the North Coast Harbor.

But unlike castles built by the child on the beach who often can't dig fast enough to stop nature from washing away the hard work, Cleveland's new foundation is securely in place.

Browns President and CEO Carmen Policy initially was skeptical about the openings in three corners of Cleveland Browns Stadium but soon fell in love with them, saying they brought the outside into the stadium, and the inside of the stadium to the outside.

There's no place like home

BY STEVE HERRICK

Although there was some debate about where to build the new Cleveland Browns Stadium, the only site seriously considered was the lakefront location where fans had watched the likes of Otto Graham, Marion Motley and Jim Brown.

Several questions were raised when the original Browns franchise moved to Baltimore following the 1995 season. The most critical question — about whether the city would get another team — was answered on February 8, 1996, when an agreement was worked out between the city and the NFL that would allow Cleveland to keep the name and colors of the Browns, with the new team beginning play in 1999.

That brought on the question of where the team would play. As part of the deal, the city agreed to build a new facility that would replace ancient Cleveland Stadium, which was built in 1931. The NFL agreed to loan the city $48 million toward construction of the new stadium. The remaining cost was financed by taxpayer money. Cuyahoga County voters extended the tax on alcohol and cigarettes on November 7, 1995, which, ironically, was the day after Art Modell announced he was moving his team to Baltimore. That tax originally helped finance the Gateway sports complex, which opened in 1994. Gateway houses Jacobs Field, where the Cleveland Indians play, and Gund Arena, the home of the Cleveland Cavaliers.

Because of the tight deadline and cost considerations, the city didn't have much time to make a decision on the location of the Browns' new stadium.

Cleveland Mayor Michael White and the NFL preferred the existing site from the very beginning. At the request of Cleveland City Council, a 45-day site-review process was conducted soon after the agreement was reached with the NFL. Some council members thought the lakefront site could be better utilized for residential development or for tourist and visitor purposes. White and the council appointed a six-member committee to investigate possible sites.

Other than the site of the old stadium, the only plausible alternative was a 60-acre site of railroad property located south of Gateway. That property was offered by Norfolk Southern Corp.

Access to the railroad's site would have caused a problem. It is cut off from downtown by highways and would have required new inter-

Demolition of Municipal Stadium began in November 1996, almost a year after the Browns played their final game there on December 17, 1995. The stadium, which opened in 1931, was home to the Browns for their first 50 years and will always have a special place in the hearts of Browns fans.

changes and access for pedestrians. Tracks from the area's Rapid Transit Authority cut through the site and the stadium would have to have been built over them.

Environmental concerns were also factored in. The Norfolk Site would have needed an extensive study, soil testing and possible cleanup.

The majority of fans were in favor of rebuilding on the old site. Fans thought it held a lot of memories from watching Browns games over the years. Other issues, such as familiarity with how to reach the stadium and where to park, were important for fans.

The committee recommended the best place for the new stadium would be on the lakefront site. The City Planning Commission also endorsed the plan, and the decision was announced on April 24, 1996.

In February of that year, White briefly considered making the new facility a domed stadium/convention center. That idea was quickly abandoned because it would have cost an estimated $80 million more to build a dome and White didn't think it would be possible to raise that much money. Plus, the dome's construction would have delayed the team's return until the 2000 or 2001 season. The city's agreement with the league allowed Cleveland to push back the arrival of the team until 2001, but that would not have been accepted very well by the fans.

Demolition of the old stadium began in November of 1996. Ground for the new stadium was broken on May 16, 1997. Cleveland Browns Stadium, which has a seating capacity of 73,200, was built at an estimated cost of $283 million.

Fans found many ways to
pay their respects to the
old stadium.

Stadium by HOK is A-OK

BY FRED GREETHAM

The stadium superstructure contains 5,300 tons — or 10,600,000 pounds — of reinforced steel. The stadium, which is 933 feet wide and 695 feet long, is 171 feet tall at its highest point.

When the project was started, it was hard to imagine a state-of-the-art facility rising out of the rubble of the old Cleveland Municipal Stadium. The task of designing Cleveland Browns Stadium was assigned to HOK Sports Facilities Group, which is no stranger to Cleveland. HOK was the firm that designed and supervised the building of Jacobs Field.

HOK Sport is the nation's largest and most prolific architectural firm in the planning, design and renovation of sports facilities. The company employs more than 320 architects, planners and support personnel dedicated to sports architecture. The firm has been involved in more than 500 sports projects and has been associated with the NFL for 25 years.

HOK Sport is a leader in the design of NFL facilities, with more than 80 football projects on its resume. The firm has worked with 29 football franchises and has designed the facilities for the Buccaneers, Ravens, Redskins, Panthers, Rams, Jaguars and Dolphins. Its engineers are in the process of designing the new stadiums for the Titans, Steelers and Patriots.

When HOK Sports Facilities Group was given the opportunity to build the new home of the Browns, it had a mandate: create a modern

Mayor White briefly considered a domed stadium, but the cost would have been too high and could have delayed the Browns' return until 2001.

stadium that combined heritage and high technology. Also, the firm had the challenge of creating a memorable building that captures the spirit of the city and its people. The finished product is a Cleveland Browns Stadium that brings together elements of past and present.

"The site offered a definite direction regarding material and esthetic, and the HOK design team focused on three profoundly significant contextual influences: the lake and shipping industry to the north, the North Coast Harbor to the east, and the city skyline to the south," Senior Project Manager Jim Chibnall said. "To the north, the lake and shipping area leave a lasting image of the industry that shaped Cleveland. The structure of the stadium takes a cue from the functional simplicity of the huge cranes that emptied their holds at port.

"We also considered both the Rock and Roll Hall of Fame and the Great Lakes Science center in the North Coast Harbor area. The facility responds with a series of boldly organized seating forms, each responding to its context and use. The "Dawg Pound" was designed similar to the former end-zone seating area known as the 'Dawg Pound' in the old Cleveland Stadium. It was designed for its very distinct fans.

"To the south, the city skyline provides a dramatic backdrop for the facility," Chibnall said. "The arrangement of the seating to the south takes advantage of the skyline, providing the majority of fans with a striking view. This creates a strong, almost physical connection to the city and community. In essence, the stadium is more than just a facility, it is a pivotal part of a greater whole."

Chibnall was the project designer for Jacobs Field, which won the prestigious American Institute of Architects Honor Award in 1995.

"At the start of the project, I became aware of the profound sense of loss the city of Cleveland and Browns fans everywhere felt with the departure of their team," Jack Boyle, HOK Sport Project Manager said. "I am proud and excited that HOK Sport played a part in the return of the Browns to the community. My hope is the Browns fans feel proud

The stadium as it
appeared in early 1999.

"I think the whole building has a significant 'wow' factor."

— JACK BOYLE, HOK PROJECT MANAGER

of their new stadium and understand the more than three years of efforts by the thousands of people responsible for its design and construction."

The uniqueness of Cleveland Browns Stadium is the fact that it is a one-of-a-kind structure.

"One of the greatest challenges of football stadium design is the task of making the building responsive to the site," HOK Project Designer Ivar Krasinski said. "In the past, facilities tended to be giant concrete doughnuts separated from their surroundings by a fence and walls. These enclosed buildings had no connection to the city around them, much less their immediate neighborhood. Made of materials entirely foreign to the context, and often out of scale, football stadiums tended to make bad neighbors."

HOK Sport Facilities Group is good at what it does. Based in Kansas City, Missouri, the company not only has the monopoly in designing new NFL stadiums, it provides the same services for college football stadiums as well as Major League Baseball stadiums.

The designers of Cleveland Browns Stadium wanted the facility to fit in well with the other buildings in the area.

"In the Cleveland Browns Stadium, the HOK Sport design team's act of cutting three huge notches into the bowl was the first step in bringing this potential monolith down to the human level," Krasinski said. "These fissures reveal the inside of the building to the passerby year-round. City space outside and football space inside freely mingle with each other. The materials and details used in the finishes are a direct response to the buildings and structures surrounding the site, from the museums on the east side to the unloading equipment (including the historic grasshopper cranes) on the west. Browns Stadium is filled with architectural, spatial and planning gestures that reach out to its neighbors."

rowns NFL Football Stadium 🏈

G AUGUST 1999

"The arrangement of the seating to the south takes advantage of the skyline, providing the majority of fans with a striking view. This creates a strong, almost physical connection to the city and community."

— JIM CHIBNALL, HOK SENIOR PROJECT MANAGER

Even though the company has been involved in many stadiums, those at HOK Sport still felt a sense of satisfaction when fans first saw the finished product.

"I am looking forward to observing the fans' reactions to their new stadium, to see how they respond to the increased amenities not found in Municipal Stadium," Boyle said. "I enjoy listening to candid reactions of fans when they see the new restrooms, concession stands, concourses and seating. I think the whole building has a significant 'wow' factor."

PAGES 70 AND 71: The stadium as it appeared on October 25, 1998.

RIGHT: "Cutting three huge notches into the bowl," observed HOK designer IVAR Krasinski, "was the first step in bringing this potential monolith down to the human level."

"It's in our blood. Like Louisiana has
gumbo, we have football."

—CHRIS SPIELMAN, ON THE IMPORTANCE OF FOOTBALL TO OHIO.

The Big Board

BY RICH EXNER

Sometimes distance makes size tough to fully comprehend. The video boards, like about everything else in Cleveland Browns Stadium, look big. Really big.

But since you probably haven't had the chance to stand next them, consider this: each screen is nearly as tall as a three-story house. They are so wide that the fastest Browns would need about three and one-half seconds to run from one end to the other.

What's more, nearly three Sony Jumbotrons the size of the one in Jacobs Field would fit inside each screen at Cleveland Browns Stadium. ➤

PAGES 74 AND 75:
Workers install seats in June 1999.

PAGES 78 AND 79: Players warm up before the Opening Night game on September 12, 1999.

At 27 feet high and 94 feet wide, the video boards perched above row 45 in both ends of the stadium are the largest in the National Football League.

But all the size in the world wouldn't matter if the new boards were not packed with clarity and substance. A staff of more than 25 people handle the substance.

Five wide-screen cameras are spotted throughout the stadium. Programming decisions are made from a control room filled with video monitors and computers, next to the press box on the southwest side of the stadium.

The Browns like to call what they do "The Best Scoreboard Show in the World."

Sometimes each board is broken into three separate screens to show highlights and action from around the league. Other times, the entire screen is used for wide-angle action. And, on occasion, messages streak across the screens.

The versatility and clarity are made possible by the latest technology from Daktronics of Brookings, South Dakota. Founded in 1968 by two electrical engineering professors, the company has become a world leader in providing electronic scoreboards and large-screen video boards everywhere from the voting chamber in the Michigan Statehouse to the Mariners' new baseball stadium in Seattle.

"Cleveland is a great sports town with great fans," Daktronics project manager Dan Chase said. "This is a state-of-the-art system that is clearly one of the best in the National Football League and all of sports."

The company is in a position to know. Daktronics products are found in the homes of NFL teams, 16 Major League Baseball teams, nine NHL teams and eight NBA teams.

Unlike the picture screen on your home TV, the video boards at the stadium use a combination of red, green and blue LEDs for each pixel, or picture element.

The scoreboards were just beginning to take shape in June 1999, two months before the first preseason game.

If you ever sat in the Stadium and wondered why the picture was so clear, even from the opposite end zone, think about this: each screen has 1.8 million LEDs, or more than 700 for every square foot of board space.

Daktronics first introduced its ProStar LED video technology in 1997 and it quickly became the new standard for large-screen video displays. By the time Browns Stadium opened in August 1999, the company had sold more than 110 of the screens.

In addition to the video boards, there are message centers and advertising panels on the two end-zone scoreboards, message boards on the sides of the stadium, two delay-of-game clocks and six locker room clocks.

And, just in case you're out of view of the large video screens, there are 1,200 television monitors throughout the Stadium.

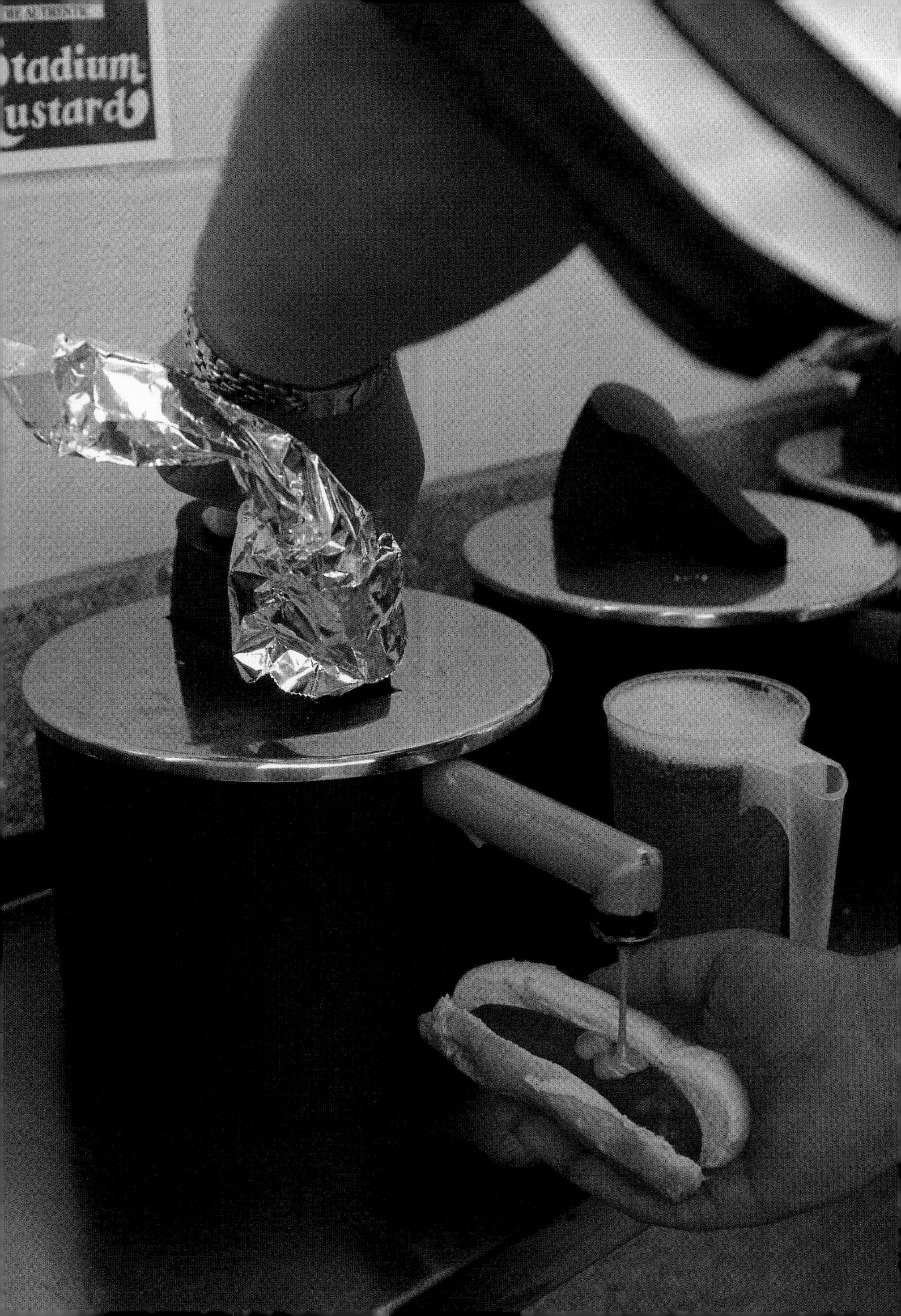
Stadium
ustard

Stadium Mustard still cuts it

BY DAN COUGHLIN

Public venues often can be identified by characteristic smells. The lobbies of neighborhood theaters smell of popcorn. Old hotels are musty. Airplanes smell of people in a hurry. The scent of fresh fish permeated the old Captain Frank's Restaurant at the foot of the East Ninth Street pier.

The original Cleveland Municipal Stadium smelled of mustard.

On David Dwoskin's first visit to Cleveland Municipal Stadium in the 1950s, his first sensory experience was the smell.

"It was not a smell," Dwoskin insists. "It was an aroma. You could smell the mustard in the concourses, and it made you want a hot dog."

The old Stadium, which opened in July 1931, was a simple horseshoe design. It had a lower concourse and an upper deck concourse, one above the other, which ran without interruption the entire circumference of the horseshoe.

Because the lower concourse was completely enclosed except for tunnels and walkways to the seats, odors were confined. There was no escape for the tantalizing vapors emitted by plastic, one-gallon jars of mustard at condiment shelves, which flanked each concession stand.

A Cleveland Stadium hot dog was more than a snack. It was an experience. The buns were steamed and the wiener itself was thin. It

The Browns preserved one of the best parts of the past by continuing to serve Stadium Mustard.

"I put my two kids through college and paid for their weddings on Stadium Mustard..."

snapped when you bit into it. Sometimes the tiny string was still attached to one end of the wiener.

But what set the hot dog apart from any other was the mustard. Vendors in the stands would not even ask if you wanted mustard. You got it. Your hot dog came with mustard dripping from both ends.

This was not the funny yellow mustard you got at Yankee Stadium and Coney Island. Cleveland Stadium mustard was brown and thick. It dripped but it did not run. In the entire United States of America, it was available only in Cleveland Stadium. On each gallon jar was affixed a small, white label, barely bigger than a postage stamp, which said in black letters, "mustard."

It had no other identifying mark. It had no brand name, no manufacturer, no list of ingredients.

Clevelanders referred to it as "Stadium Mustard."

In the typical gourmet delicatessen of the time, you could find dozens of mustards, but none even closely approximated the flavor of Stadium Mustard. Because it was not available in stores, people grew desperate for it. Housewives would conceal tiny jars in their purses, which they would fill at the concession stands when they thought they were not observed, and smuggle them home to their own refrigerators.

Dwoskin, the son of a kosher butcher in the suburbs of Cleveland Heights, was destined to follow in his father's footsteps. At the age of 19, he was already working full time in the butcher shop.

But in October 1962, as the Jewish holidays approached and the Browns were preparing to play a nondescript young team from Dallas called the Cowboys, Dwoskin made the decision that changed his life.

It was 11 o'clock at night. He was holding a chicken with his left hand and his right hand was inside it. He looked at his friend, Larry Wasserman, and said, "I don't want to be a butcher."

Dwoskin went into the clothing business. Every time he sold a brown suit, he thought, "this is a good color. It will not show the stain

Cleveland Browns
Stadium has 43
permanent and 61
portable concession
stands.

of Stadium Mustard when it drops on you."

Needless to say, Dwoskin was obsessed.

In 1970 he approached a small Cleveland food brokerage and proposed that he take Stadium Mustard on the road.

Stadium Mustard is made in Chicago, according to an old German recipe brought to this country generations ago. Its only customer was Cleveland Stadium until Dwoskin came along.

He designed a label and had the manufacturer package it in small jars, which Dwoskin took around to stores and supermarkets in the Cleveland area. It turned up in the Orange Bowl because the concessionaire there was a former Clevelander who also loved Stadium Mustard.

By the 1980s, Dwoskin acquired exclusive rights to Stadium Mustard and quit the clothing business. He traveled the country promoting a condiment. If a guy named Morton could eke out a living on salt and Durkee could manage on pepper, Dwoskin would make his mark with mustard.

Soon Stadium Mustard was in several minor league ballparks, college stadiums and high school fields across the country. It even was added to the Hubert H. Humphrey Metrodome in Minneapolis.

But Dwoskin's heart was broken in 1994 when the Indians moved into Jacobs Field and did not include him. The Indians bought a name, Ballpark Mustard, similar but not identical.

"Similar but not as good," says Dwoskin.

That is his opinion and he is entitled to it. After all, he has defended his position for half a century.

Dwoskin's heart was broken again when the Browns moved to Baltimore, the stadium went dark and later was torn down. Stadium Mustard was a mustard without a stadium. Dwoskin felt like a man without a home.

In the summer of 1999, however, the new Browns management made one of the most important decisions of its regime.

"They told me I'd be back, and I'm elated," said Dwoskin. "It's resuming a 50-year tradition."

The new Cleveland Browns Stadium ordered 500 gallons of Stadium Mustard for the first preseason game. By the time the Steelers arrived for the first official game, Dwoskin had delivered another 500-gallon order.

"I put my two kids through college and paid for their weddings on Stadium Mustard," says Dwoskin. "I have received thousands of letters from people all over the world looking for Stadium Mustard, from Alaska, Germany, the Himalayas. Somebody sent me a picture of a Chinese soldier standing at the Great Wall of China holding a jar of Stadium Mustard. I even have a Web site, www.stadiummustard.com."

The man behind the mask

BY RICH EXNER

John "Big Dawg" Thompson might be the most photographed fan in all of professional sports.

From his customary post in the front row of the bleachers at old Cleveland Stadium, his getup became recognizable to most any person who ever walked through the gates or caught more than a snippet of Browns action on television.

If there was a play worth rooting for, there was the huge man who became known as the Big Dawg barking away in his hard hat, dog mask and No. 98 jersey— giant brown-and-orange dog bone in hand.

Then an amazing thing happened. His celebrity status grew even after the Browns left town in 1995.

He was in Atlanta for an NFL owners meeting in an attempt to convince the owners to block the move of the team. He was on Capitol Hill testifying before the U.S. House Judiciary Committee that something should be done to slow franchise moves.

He became the target of autograph seekers and picture takers most anywhere he donned his famous mask.

Most of the time, he wasn't asking to be at center stage. He was politely saying OK when asked. "I didn't elect myself to go to Congress," Thompson says. "I was chosen by my congressman."

By the time the Browns returned to the field, he was marketing Big

LEFT: Big Dawg was just a salesman named John Thompson until he decided to put on the mask, almost by accident.

PAGES 92 AND 93: Browns players quickly resumed the tradition of greeting fans in the Dawg Pound.

"I love my Browns just like everyone else does," says Thompson, a computer-supply salesmen during the day. "I'm going to love them until I die."

Dawg Crunch cereal, with a portion of the profits earmarked for charity, figuring he might as well take advantage of the opportunity.

And it all happened because of what Thompson says was a "crazy, wacky, situation" in 1985, soon after the talented and flashy cornerback duo of Hanford Dixon and Frank Minnifield gave birth to the idea of putting a dog identity on the team with plain helmets.

Thompson, 25 at the time and a lifelong Browns fan from the West Side of Cleveland, says it would be a mistake to think there was some deep thinking involved.

"A Saturday afternoon, a couple of beers, a costume shop, a dog mask and you've got it," Thompson says.

Even his trademark No. 98 jersey carries no special significance.

"That's the biggest jersey that was available when I bought it," recalls Thompson, who tipped the scales at 350 pounds when the 1999 season began.

By 1986, he was barking away through what he remembers as his biggest high and lowest low as a fan, outside losing the team altogether. That was the season the Browns rallied in the playoffs to beat the Jets in overtime before losing in overtime the following week in the John Elway Drive game seconds short of a Super Bowl trip.

He describes the whole Big Dawg thing as "completely mind-blowing." After all, who would think any fan, no matter how unique among almost 80,000 in the old stadium, could take on such a celebrity status?

"But the most important thing is to be able to look out on the field and see my orange and brown back," says Thompson now that he again is settling into the bleachers on Sunday afternoons.

The night the stadium opened, so many fans mobbed their fellow fan outside the stadium that he was late getting to his seat. Inside, it's difficult for him to watch the action sometimes because so many people want autographs or pictures.

But he is as patient and as friendly as a big puppy.

Big Dawg with his daughter, Megan, at the Hall of Fame Game.

About all you'll hear him complain about are lousy penalty calls or the lack of a vendor nearby. What fan wouldn't do that?

He says it is tough at times because of the demands, but he made himself a promise not to be anything but a regular fan.

"I love my Browns just like everyone else does," says Thompson, a computer-supply salesman during the day. "I'm going to love them until I die."